Think Inside the Box

Discover the exceptional business inside your
organization

Tim Nelson

Jim McGee

WCG Press, Winnetka, IL

WCG Press

Winnetka Consulting Group, Inc.

Winnetka, IL

info@winnetkaconsultinggroup.com

insidethe8020box.com

www.wcgpress.com

www.winnetkaconsultinggroup.com

Printed in the United States of America

ISBN-13 (pbk): 978-0-9892503-0-6

ISBN-13 (ePub): 978-0-9892503-1-3

ISBN-13 (mobi/Kindle): 978-0-9892503-2-0

2013-11-16

Prologue
A Twenty Million Dollar Lesson

Midwest Industrial Packaging (MIP) was founded in early 1987. It was a classic startup in a market too small to attract a large company but large enough to support a healthy medium sized business. The market for industrial packaging products and materials wasn't glamorous but MIP provided products that every business needed.

Over the next thirteen years, MIP grew to become the world's largest simple packaging tool company selling over 100 different products to 1,000 customers in 44 countries. Forty of these tools were manufactured; the remaining items were purchased overseas and resold. In 2000, MIP generated $7 million in annual sales, 4% in operating income, turned inventory 3 ½ times per year, and employed 52 people.

MIP's operation was textbook manufacturing, as taught in most business schools, with machining, assembly, quality control, shipping, and receiving. Products were manufactured in batches to make more efficient use of manufacturing assets and complicated set-ups. The Quality Control department inspected incoming raw materials and parts, inspected the first products off the line during batch production, and checked outgoing products before shipment. Materials handlers pulled parts and material from stock to prepare batches for assembly, monitored and tracked key parts during assembly, and periodically worked to get rapid delivery of key components when a shortage threatened to slow up or stop a production batch.

In 2000, MIP was acquired by a Fortune 500 conglomerate, Illinois Tool Works (ITW). MIP rounded out ITW's product line as a value brand. MIP products could also be offered to customers as a way to generate incremental sales and income from existing accounts. As part of the acquisition agreement, MIP continued to operate as an independent business unit. Multiple opportunities to significantly streamline and improve MIP's operations were identified during the acquisition review and due diligence.

MIP's founder and staff began to learn, adopt, apply, and modify the tools, techniques, and methods described in the book that follows.

What were the results at MIP?

Over the next seven years, operating income rose from 4% to 28%. Inventory turns rose from 3½ to 12 times per year. Revenue per employee went from $143,000/year to $435,000/year. The valuation of the business increased $20 million over the price originally paid to MIP's founder. All of this was accomplished with the original management team, the same resources, and the same customer base. There was no grand change in strategy, no radical innovations in technology, no clever financial engineering.

The methods and practices applied at MIP worked as effectively as they had wherever else they have been applied. The playbook is not difficult or secret. It does require focus and discipline. The following chapters map the principles, practices, analyses, and tools that will allow any organization to travel this path. This book is designed to allow any organization to travel this path without the $20 million tuition bill.

Contents

PART 1
ACCEPTING
CONTINUAL CHANGE

CHAPTER 1
MANAGING IN A GLOBAL ECONOMY

We operate in economic reality, which isn't always obvious watching the nightly news, reading the mainstream business press, browsing the list of business books on Amazon, or listening to typical coffee shop conversations. The problems and issues discussed seem grander than those we face daily in our own organizations. Proposals abound to redesign or replace fundamental elements of the economy. Everyone has an opinion on what's wrong with the economy and how to fix it; if only someone would put them in charge.

These economic debates are generally entertaining and sometimes thought-provoking. Previously, they have had little bearing on the routine decisions that managers make. Today, we live and compete in a complex, multi-dimensional, and dynamic world. Good business decisions incorporate the state of the economic environment and that environment has become global for even the smallest enterprise. Global issues are as pertinent and immediate as any local business event. What the local hardware store stocks is affected by the Home Depot down the road and the web retailer who stocks the exact, 5-year old, discontinued, cabinet hinge that just broke in the kitchen. Managers and executives in every size organization must develop a better grasp of their company's larger economic context or be overrun by it.

All organizations are confronted with too few resources to address every problem and opportunity that the current economy presents. A fundamental task of management is to decide where to focus and how to allocate scare resources to real problems and opportunities. In today's world, management does not have the luxury of making these decisions only during an annual budget cycle. What were once stable, correct answers to routine corporate planning questions, must now evolve continually just as the competitive landscape itself changes and morphs. No matter how smart the practices or powerful the tools, answers have a shelf life and that shelf life grows shorter every year. **Dealing with continual change has brought its own host of problems and opportunities. It demands a new, unacknowledged, skill set.**

The approach we describe in this book helps decision makers identify and rank opportunities to improve organizational performance. This approach:

- Is data driven, using data already available in the organization.

- Relies on a well-established rule-of-thumb (the 80/20 rule or Pareto principle) to determine focus and attention.

- Anchors analysis in the fundamental elements of any economic organization; products and services and the customers who buy them.

- Does not depend on rare or unusual skills, techniques, or technology. This is proven technology, readily available and in use in many organizations.

- Adapts simply to new data as it becomes available. As initiatives come online and show results, those results can be readily cycled back through the process.

- Has a proven track record; applied to over 850 businesses acquired and integrated in one Fortune 150 company, ITW, which has consistently produced superior results.

80/20 Thinking and Quadrant Mapping

The 80/20 Rule (also known as the Pareto Principle)[1] crops up empirically in many settings and circumstances including business. Business organizations, for example, find that approximately 80% of their revenue comes from just the top 20% of customers. Similarly, 20% of products account for 80% of total sales. This skewed distribution appears so consistently in economic environments that it offers a simple, data-driven, non-controversial basis for directing managerial focus. A clear basis to identify the customers and products that are most important economically to an organization eliminates many unproductive arguments. This allows managerial decisions to be grounded in empirical data rather than just experience and intuition.

Preparing an 80/20 analysis once required a significant commitment of technology and analytical resources. Collecting and scrubbing the relevant cost accounting data occupied weeks of time for a good size team of expensive consultants. Consolidating the data and preparing the basic 80/20 analysis took additional time and expertise. This type of analysis involved sorting your customers, products, and inventory based on applying the 80/20 rule to separate the core drivers of your business.

Today, the wide availability of enterprise software and accounting systems combined with the data manipulation and analytical tools of spreadsheet programs bring the mechanics of 80/20 analysis within easy reach of all but the smallest organizations. Many organizations struggle to develop and deploy a systematic, coherent process for employing existing systems and tools. Most executives, with deep knowledge of their institution, can, with proper coaching, produce a much more powerful analysis of their own organization than an outside consulting team. Doing the work yourself leads to stronger, more insightful analysis. This book provides a step-by-step process to use in the application of 80/20 and furthermore provides you with additional tools to use to help transform your business.

A basic 80/20 analysis of customers or products is revealing in its own right. However, the unique process, as outlined in this book, of combining the customer and product analyses amplifies its power to generate focus on the core drivers of a business. When you overlay the 80/20 analysis of customers on a simultaneous 80/20 analysis of products you produce a matrix with four quadrants; creating a Quadrant (or "Quad") Map. The Quads, shown below in Exhibit 1, can be labeled:

1. **Core**: the sale of your top products to your top customers. 60-70% of an organization's total gross margin typically comes from the Core.

2. **Supporting Products**: the sale of your remaining products (the bottom 80%) to your top customers.

3. **Benefactor** Customers: the sale of your top 20% products to the rest of your customer base

4. **Residual**: the sale of your least profitable 80% products to your least profitable 80% customers.

Exhibit 1
Quad Map Structure

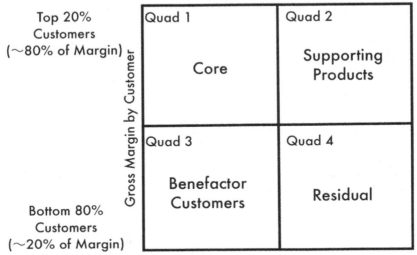

Top 20% Customers (~80% of Margin)

Gross Margin by Customer

Quad 1 Core	**Quad 2** Supporting Products
Quad 3 Benefactor Customers	**Quad 4** Residual

Bottom 80% Customers (~20% of Margin)

Gross Margin by Product

Top 20% SKUs (~80% of Margin)   **Bottom 80% SKUs (~20% of Margin)**

An initial mapping process can be conducted in a period of a few days to a few weeks. The mapping can be done internally using the data already being collected in existing accounting and information systems. The result is a treasure map, a guide to the most promising places to look for opportunity. This process categorizes each product and customer into a quadrant, isolating them so that you can "think inside the box" to maximize the value of each aspect of your business.

Structure of the Book

In the remaining chapters of Part 1 we delve more deeply into the challenges of today's economic environment especially the challenges of globalization and continual, dynamic change. We explore the scale and scope of what we have been calling the "neglected middle". We discuss issues that affect small and medium sized businesses. We look at why this slice of the economy attracts the attention and focus of Private Equity investors and why it is likely to continue to do so. And, we look at the challenges and opportunities to create significant change and improvement in these organizations.

In Parts 2 and 3 we explore the process and techniques of preparing a Quad Map and its use to set and drive the agenda of multiple improvement efforts. Many tactical and strategic tools are useful for tackling specific issues and challenges within an organization. Their value is amplified when they are organized and matched against problems in a systematic, but flexible way. That value can also be squandered if the tools are applied to problems capriciously. We lay out the considerations for coordinating and sequencing the use of the tools across organizational silos so that efforts in different areas of the company reinforce and complement one another.

In Part 4 we explore the challenges of moving from insight to sustained organizational change. Small teams can perform the analytical work to identify promising opportunities. However, the team insight that occurs during this process is not sufficient to support the larger task of changing organizational practices and processes to support the new environment. This section explores how to institutionalize these practices and processes, so that organizations can continue to evolve and adapt to their competitive environment.

All of the individual parts of this book demonstrate that organizations can cultivate and develop methods, with existing resources, to implement change. The methods expressed in this book will ultimately enable you to unearth increased value and productivity for your company.

CHAPTER 2
MANAGING THE TRANSITION FROM INSIGHT TO CHANGE

The Neglected Middle

According to the US Small Business Administration[2] there are 28 million small businesses in the United States, "small" being defined as 499 employees or fewer. There is over $7.8 trillion dollars worth of revenue and 42 million employees tied to these small businesses (35.4% of the US work force). Small businesses are importing and exporting, competing internationally, working with government bureaucracy, complying with regulatory agencies, filing payroll and corporate taxes and just trying to survive. Small does not mean simple.

The very small and very large organizations tend to garner most of the media and academic attention. Start-ups with a unique and unusual product are a special breed. Their focus is less about maximization of their existing product offering and more about survival and building growth and infrastructure. Large enterprises are maddeningly complex but generally have the resources and talent they need to identify and address their challenges. Organizations at each end of the size spectrum get the press. Their problems are chronicled and catalogued. Researchers and consultants mine them for insight and opportunity.

What enterprises in the middle have in common is a thinner managerial bench, real constraints on problem solving resources, complex problems, and morphing opportunities. This middle range of enterprises rarely gets the attention it deserves. Industrial behemoths have perfected their ability to stay visible in the media, as have the newest, technologically driven start-ups in places such as Silicon Valley, Route 128, and Seattle. The neglected, or at least overlooked, middle is equally important even when it borders on the invisible.

The neglected middle is the primary focus of this book. There is one place, however, where the neglected middle is not so neglected. This is where most private equity (PE) firms make their living. The very existence of the private equity market provides economic confirmation that opportunities exist to improve the performance and value of midlevel businesses.

The Role of Private Equity in the Middle

There are over 2,600 private equity (PE) firms in the market today.[3] These companies invested over $144 Billion in 2011 alone with $1.7 trillion over the last 10 years.[4] Some private equity firms specialize in purchasing capital hungry businesses and boosting their growth. Others focus on businesses that are bankrupt and in need of a complete makeover. However, most of the opportunities involve purchasing underperforming middle market businesses and increasing their value by transforming the organization and its operations. Many large, publicly traded companies such as ITW, Danaher, Marmon Group, and GE operate in a similar manner with longer time horizons for holding the asset. Both Private Equity and these larger corporations have had tremendous success by targeting enterprises operating in the neglected middle.

The owners and employees of the targeted organizations do not always benefit from the value created from transformation. PE firms may appear to bring some secret sauce to the purchase of a business. Short term cost savings, financial leveraging cheap bank debt, and other techniques can quickly boost accounting profits. The most effective PE firms implement new operating processes, policies, and lean practices that focus a business around the business's core customers and products.

We wrote this book, in part, to help the business owner, general manager, or middle manager apply many of the very same techniques to directly tap the value existing in their businesses today. We have been on both sides of the equation: selling businesses that were subsequently transformed or acting as outside consultants leading the transformation. We have walked in your shoes.

What we offer is a proven, data-driven, process to identify and implement the most effective improvements to your business. The process does not require elaborate technology or unusual skills. With knowledge, management can partner effectively with outside help. Instead of defending the status quo against external threats, management can unleash and reap the full potential of the business.

Why this Book Offers Better Insight

This book is rooted in a data driven process of tangible steps that allow you to systematically analyze and improve your business. We discuss lean practices and principles that you likely already know but also provide a process to systematically execute them. We focus on being pragmatic. A quote from Jack Welch's book, *Winning,* is an example of the type of advice we find in too many books written by prominent, successful CEO's. Welch, former CEO of General Electric, advises "have a positive attitude and spread it around, never let yourself be a victim, and for goodness' sake – have fun."[5] How is a business owner in the neglected middle expected to make practical use of this type of advice?

Previously, only the largest consulting companies offered these techniques and only the largest organizations could afford the cost. Now the value developed by these techniques can stay within the organization and its creators.

What makes this feasible? Several trends have converged to make this possible:

- Business owners and managers are more educated. They have a global perspective and the ability to analyze information.

- Sophisticated data analysis is readily available and accessible to the average organization. Technology has allowed for the extensive collection and analysis of data. Small and mid-size accounting packages are more sophisticated and capable of manipulating data easily. Spreadsheet software, such as Microsoft's Excel, has pushed data analysis to the masses and the ability to present complex information in revealing ways has improved dramatically.

- Understanding data to successfully execute change has never been easier or more cost effective. Every business we have ever taken this process has experienced a significant increase in their operating income.

Still, this is not a cookie cutter approach. While the process and techniques are the same the solution for each company is unique. The presence of management leading the process will inherently create better insight and stronger, more permanent change.

Commitment to change is built on engagement in the work

A central lesson in change management is that the commitment to change follows engagement in the process, not the other way around. Participating in the planning and execution of the change creates the commitment to the process. The adage that successful change efforts depend on executive commitment and support misses this essential criticality of engaging the rank-and-file. The rank-and-file in most organizations is routinely ignored in the transformation process. Employees watch what managers do, and where they are visibly engaged. Often employees finesse their way through the "trend-du-jour" and simply keep doing things the way they have always been done. The secret to success boils down to understanding whose engagement matters most and getting those players involved. Get the right executives, leaders, and employees engaged and the necessary personal and organizational commitment and energy follows. Fail to widely involve people in the process and no amount of rational argument, exhortation, or compulsion will lead to any degree of change.

The initial 80/20 analysis and quadrant mapping engages the necessary individuals in a simple, low risk, low commitment process. The initial steps ground the organization in the existing data and lend themselves to early engagement and acceptance. **This first step of this process is unusual compared to other transformational techniques because it is so inclusive and ramps up so innocuously.**

The mechanics of filling a spreadsheet with gross margin data by customer or product and sorting the results from high to low are simple and difficult to dispute. Maintain a running tally of cumulative gross margin in a separate column and the point where 80% of total gross margin has been accounted for will be immediately evident. If you've been on the team doing the work, you will get a much more powerful "Aha!" moment when you see what a small group the top 20% of your customers constitutes. The emotional impact when you see a favorite customer or product far down the list in the 80% who contribute little or no benefit to the organization is far more powerful and motivating when you have prepared the spreadsheet yourself than when reviewing the same result on a slide in some consultant's presentation.

There is something both grounding and energizing in scrolling through a spreadsheet prepared with internal data by internal staff and seeing the point where products cost more than they generate in margin. The sheer number of products that fall below this threshold can be very sobering. The facts conveyed from the data make it harder to remain emotionally attached to a favorite product or customer that is not bringing any economic benefit to the organization. Being part of the team that sifted through the evidence is a critical step in accepting the message and acting on it.

Engaging the people who truly understand the business in the process makes it easy to see good improvements and possible to discover potentially game changing opportunities. The process is as much about execution as it is about analysis. People need to believe the evidence. When they believe, they will be more likely to abandon their myopic, local perspective of their function or department and start to focus on the company as a whole.

Improving Systems rather than Silos

There are many tools and approaches to improve performance. Most have value in the right situation. All too often, tools are peddled as silver bullets, magical answers to any and all problems. Lasting success, however, flows to those organizations that integrate "we've always done it this way" with "there has to be a better way." This synthesis depends on learning to see the business as a coherent system of interconnected parts.

Organizations always complain about silos (marketing, sales, accounting, production), but silos are the inevitable result of pursuing efficiency and effectiveness. Silos can't be eliminated but they must be managed if organizations are to succeed. Tools and approaches that optimize individual silos do so at the expense of the system as a whole. You cannot optimize the system as a whole unless you deliberately and intentionally sub-optimize the components. Unless you are evaluating and making tradeoffs across the system, you are not managing. The central tradeoff in all economic organizations is between satisfying the unique requirements of each customer and seeking economies in the production and delivery of each product or service.

Separate 80/20 analyses of customers or products/services reinforce existing silos. The primary advantage of the Quad Mapping process is that it captures and highlights the tradeoffs from a systems perspective rather than individual silos. Understanding an organization's best customers or best products is valuable in its own right. However, this examination misses the complexity costs and transactional impact of marginal customers or products. A Quad Map showing both customers and products provides a guide to understand the organizational system as a whole. A Quad Map will simultaneously reveal optimizations within and between silos that amplify the value of core customers and products and unexpected opportunities that exist at the boundaries between silos. Opportunities exist in focusing on what an organization does well. They also exist in eliminating what an organization doesn't do well. Thinking inside each box creates the greatest value.

CHAPTER 3
TODAY'S ECONOMIC REALITY—GLOBAL, DYNAMIC, COMPLEX

Trends and Globalization

The broad trend toward globalization has been playing out over centuries, but accelerating in the last couple decades. The location and availability of key raw materials has driven trade since man figured out that one knife and one coconut were better than two knives alone or two coconuts alone. Differences in labor costs, skills, and resources drove outsourcing decisions. Cheap energy and transportation costs made global supply chains economical. Digitization and improved information and communications technologies made these same supply chains increasingly easier to design and manage. It is this evolving economic environment that forces companies to be more and more focused and always on their game.

The U.S.A. is the mother lode of all international markets. Every company in every single type of industry, in all 196 countries of the world, wants to sell to us. What our fellow international competitors don't realize is that the United States is also the most competitive market in the world. With our open door policies and price conscious buyers - it is competition at its best — and at its worse. The companies that succeed in surviving - just like the conclusion to Orson B. Welles's War of Worlds radio broadcast[6] - "have earned the right to be here". However, our dominant status continues to change. We are increasingly under attack from everywhere in the world. We must continually work to outperform our competitors. Where it was once just domestic competitors it is now increasingly international with everyone having your business as their primary target.

Today's environment of ubiquitous Internet connectivity and access to the global logistics networks of TNT, FedEx, and UPS make all potential competitors, suppliers, and customers effectively next-door. If these competitors' governments subsidize exports and enjoy the luxury of trade barriers protecting their domestic markets, then that is our economic reality. These major economic shifts will continue to alter the ground rules. And decisions that once seemed esoteric and removed will impact our daily lives. This is the economic reality we inhabit. It is only going to become more prominent.

If you were awake during Economics 101 you'll likely recall the notion of comparative advantage. Economies and industries succeed when they find and focus on whatever inherent advantage they possess. If your country was founded on top of diamond mines, then you go into the diamond business. You don't try to grow bananas. This advantage is not just about resources. Singapore, with few natural resources, finds its comparative advantage lies in a sophisticated and educated workforce located near the largest emerging markets on the planet. The key is successfully identifying these advantages.

In the transition to a global economy, accidental advantages and edges have faded into irrelevance. Further, most of the remaining real advantages are primarily available to individual organizations within countries. A thorough review of existing structure produces a better understanding of business drivers and competencies. It is critical that you build and defend from your comparative advantage.

In this century, global competition, fair or otherwise, will continue to supply plenty of evolutionary pressure to become "lean, sober, and smart." "Fat, drunk, and stupid" was no path to success in the movie *Animal House* yet for the second half of the 20th Century, the equivalent strategy worked moderately well for many American companies. The Quad approach presents a path to a lean, sober, and smart operation that has been tested and proven in the field.

Data and Decisions

The connections between data and decisions have been evolving in peculiar directions over the past 25 years. For some problems, hard data provides answers that are unambiguously right or wrong. Structural engineers, for example, calculate the necessary size of a structural steel beam to support the floor above your head. In other situations, recommending a book based on the buying habits of other readers leads to a demonstrable increase in sales of that book. You can use data to calculate an optimal inventory level for certain parts to keep an assembly line running with minimal risk of a stock out shutting down the line.

At one end of the spectrum, no one seems able to routinely predict the next hot fashion trend or the movements of any particular stock. However, sometimes we can make statistical predictions that help a company earn better returns on average than the market. Other times, however, there are things we cannot predict - like acts of God. There are also categories of problems where no amount of data will reveal a right answer. There was no evidence to support Sony's decision to bring the Sony Walkman to market in 1979. In fact, there was substantial evidence to argue against its decision. As Harvard Business School Professor Clay Christensen puts it "markets that don't exist can't be analyzed."[7]

These realities are among the core reasons that management is as interesting and challenging as it is. Our emphasis here is on problems where available systems provide a level of hard data. We can then incorporate that data into analyses that lead to greater insight and better decisions. For all the rhetoric about the "rational economic man" or the value of analytically based decisions, the reality of day-to-day management has not only an inescapable level of uncertainty and risk but also requires access to hard data and insight. This hard data and insight are the best tools available to navigate this new economic reality in which we all exist. It is worth understanding what we have learned about decision-making and what we have learned about the relative value of data in varying decision settings.

It's a Change, Change, Change, Change World

There seems little doubt that the economic environment is in an extended period of dynamic change. Globalization is merely one of the forces driving the pace of change. Technology, media, popular culture, literacy, public health, science, and population demographics are others. Organizations survive, thrive, and grow if they are either well adapted to their external competitive environment or have managed to exercise a significant level of control over their environment.

If you accept that the pace of change has accelerated, what does this entail for organizations? Few organizations are positioned to exercise much control over the competitive environment. Perhaps a handful of the world's largest organizations have some influence, although even giants such as BP and Exxon have discovered that their level of control is much smaller than it once was. A larger group of companies thrived during periods of what we would now deem temporary control or influence. The US auto industry, airlines, steel, and telecommunications all come to mind. Unexamined and ultimately incorrect assumptions of permanent stability led many of these organizations into bad habits and practices. Smaller organizations (relative to these giants) have rarely, if ever, had any significant degree of influence on their environment. On the other hand, many of the executives who've reached senior levels in their organizations gained much of their experience when that environment was much less volatile. Their worldview sees change as a rare event and adaptability as a synonym for lack of control.

Organizations value stability. They are built to create it, celebrate it, and reinforce it. Consider all of the clear and subtle indicators you can find in organizations about the value of stability, tradition, and history:

- Signs on the factory floor announcing "200 days without an accident"

- "Established in 1898"

- "The HP Way"

- Lapel pins celebrating 5, 10, or 20 years of service

History and precedent weigh heavily in all organizations. The more successful the organization, the more often "we've always done it that way" is a debate-ending assertion. The more experienced and successful the executive, the more often proposed ideas are dismissed with "we tried that before and it didn't work." Successfully blending stability and change is a central challenge in all organizations.

The choice is not between fossilization and chaos. It is how to best incorporate continual change in the environment and focus the organization on developing the capabilities and capacities to navigate that environment. For too many organizations, their assumptions about change and adaptability are wrong, dangerously so to many. From those who view fossilization as the greater risk, you will hear existing organizations described as dinosaurs and new practices as the small mammals destined to displace the old. From those worried about chaos, yet convinced of the need for change, you may hear references to "burning platforms."

The most dangerous assumption about organizational change is that change is a rare, disruptive event that separates long periods of stability. While that might have been somewhat true at one time, it is not today. We must treat change in a way that highlights the truths of today's world and points toward better strategies for operating in that world. We must develop and employ strategies that embrace change rather than coping with it.

Organizational scientist Peter Vaill[8] has articulated the most useful metaphor for change that we have encountered. He argues for thinking of change as a process of navigating in a world of "permanent whitewater." Both words are important to understanding how to redesign our organizations for success in this new environment. "Whitewater" because it is force, turbulence, speed, unpredictability, and hidden obstacles that characterize the new environment. Also the origins of the whitewater may be far upstream (e.g. Globalization, government policy, supply chain disruptions). "Permanent" because these characteristics are now dominant and persistent features of the environment. There is no calm water on the "other" side where we can return to our old ways if only we can hang on

14

through a short set of rapids. You either have to act on the situation in front of you or you have to hold on and ride it out. Riding it out takes a lot of effort; exhausting you, but providing little else to show for the ride.

Our choice is not whether we can withstand the battering from this whitewater environment, but whether we choose to be passive or active in our interaction with the rapids. We're going to get bruised. Our choice is to hang on for the ride or to paddle. Learning to paddle and exploiting local conditions, understanding forces that caused them, and believing that there is no calm lake or stream on the other side all constitute a better strategy. The tools and techniques we describe here fit in both a static and dynamic world. To work well in the dynamic world that business competes in today, tools must be embedded in processes and practices where they can be taken out and routinely applied to the evolving competitive environment.

Evolving understanding of human decision making

Over the last few decades, what we know about how people make decisions has mushroomed. At the same time, we have seen an exponential growth in the data that is now routinely available for our decision-making needs. Sometimes, these trends reinforce one another; at other times, they clash.

We believe in the value of evidence and analysis. We are also aware of its limits. In this book, we explore ways to leverage evidence and analysis to produce better decisions and results and ways to avoid the traps of "analysis paralysis."

There is no "one right way" to make decisions. The best you can hope to achieve is a track record of reasonable and satisfactory decisions within the constraints of the moment. We study decisions and decision making to understand how these constraints work and how we can improve our decision-making averages.

Our capacity for decision-making is based on understanding the different ways we study decisions, the differing kinds of decisions that we encounter, and the differing constraints that operate in any given situation.

The study of decisions is a subject that has occupied business researchers, economists, sociologists, psychologists, and political scientists for as long as these disciplines and their precursors have existed. All of these fields offer valuable insights. At the same time, each of these fields is complex in its own right. Each field's unique perspective shapes what is examined, valued, and seen. To understand the dynamics of these sources provides us with incremental insights about the lessons we can take away and apply in our own decision settings.

The career agendas of rising academics drive the study of decision-making as much as, or more than, mundane decision making in the real world. Academics and consultants love to study edge cases and leading edge practices. They are less interested in whether and how those techniques might matter to those who don't live on the bleeding edge but merely need to employ the science of decision making in routine matters and ordinary businesses.

What's missing?

The raw materials for analysis and insight are available. So are the basic analytical tools. What does your enterprise need to take advantage of this new reality and avoid being overrun by it? How do you successfully figure out what the market values most about your company? What are your core competencies?

First, you need an analytical roadmap. You need to know where to start, what to do next, and what comes at the end. You need this from a pragmatic point of view. You need concrete advice and simply, understandable tools that you can execute. It is helpful to get this guidance from people who have been through the process before, and like you have run and managed businesses. The rest of the book walks you through this process. While the process is the same, the answers for each company are different. The process is always iterative. Even if you don't perform a full Quad Analysis, the concepts and lean tools discussed in the book will add value.

PART 2
UNDERSTANDING THE BUSINESS, IDENTIFYING THE OPPORTUNITIES

CHAPTER 4
80/20 ANALYSIS IN ACTION–
DISSECTING THE NUMBERS

Analyzing the data that exists

The analytical process starts with a Red Light/Green Light Analysis. This provides a 10,000-foot understanding of a company by performing a straightforward 80/20 analysis of the data by customer, product, and vendor. It also serves a critical role in establishing the project team and building initial momentum for the improvement effort.

Analysis begins with gathering data from the existing systems of record used primarily in accounting to control the business operationally. This data gathering process should be completed in front of actually kicking off the 80/20 and Quad Process within your organization. Someone with relevant knowledge and experience should review the data to make certain that it makes sense. This avoids a false start due to bad data. It usually takes the accounting department two to three days at least to create the correct program to extract the pertinent data from existing systems of record.

Exhibit 2
Overview of the Analysis Process

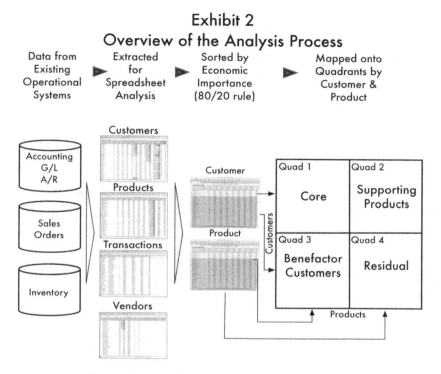

| Data from Existing Operational Systems | ▶ | Extracted for Spreadsheet Analysis | ▶ | Sorted by Economic Importance (80/20 rule) | ▶ | Mapped onto Quadrants by Customer & Product |

Information gathering starts with what we affectionately call a data dump. This information is standard accounting data and should be readily available. It requires the accounting department to extract data from existing operational and accounting systems (e.g. Sales Orders, Inventory Management, Accounts Receivable) and load the data into a spreadsheet where it can be manipulated and analyzed.

The following exhibit provides an example of the customer worksheet derived from the organization's existing operational systems. Below the sample worksheet is a list of the specific data columns that need to be extracted for customers.

Exhibit 3
Data Dump Worksheets and Columns—Sample

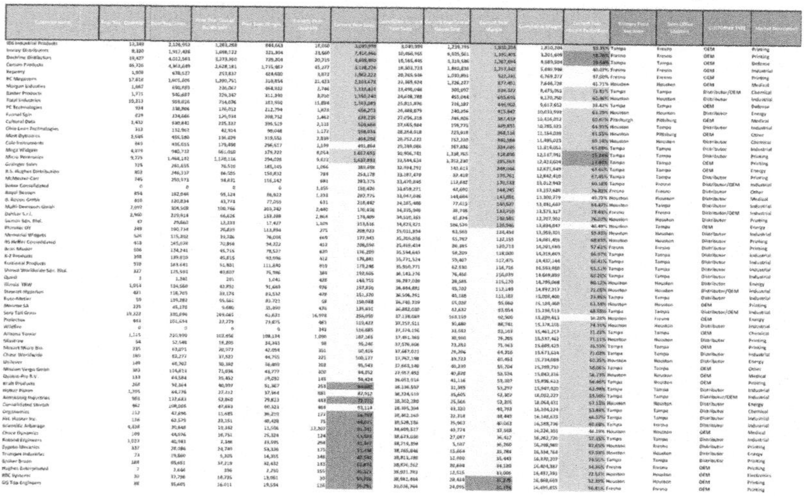

Customer Worksheet Columns

01 - Customer ID
02 - Customer Name
03 - Prior Year's Revenue
04 - Prior Year's Gross Margin
05 - Prior Year's Gross Margin %
06 - Prior Year's Quantity Sold

07 - Current Year's Revenue
08 - Current Year's Gross Margin
09 - Current Year's Gross Margin %
10 - Current Year's Quantity Sold
11 - Customer Type
12 - Market Segment
13 - Sales Office
14 - Primary Plant
15 - Material Type

A corresponding worksheet of product data also needs to be extracted from existing operational systems. The data columns of product data needed are:

- Product ID

- Product Name

- Prior Year's Revenue

- Prior Year's Gross Margin

- Prior Year's Gross Margin %

- Prior Year's Quantity Sold

- Current Year's Revenue

- Current Year's Gross Margin

- Current Year's Gross Margin %
- Current Year's Quantity Sold
- Current Year's
- End User Industry
- Material Category
- Plant Location
- Material Type

In the product and customer data dumps we are looking 24 months back. The reason to include the prior year is to make certain there haven't been major changes in product or customer. If there were, incorporate it in the analysis.

The third worksheet to create is a transactions worksheet of sales of products to customers. The data columns for the transaction worksheet are:

- Customer ID
- Customer Name
- Product ID
- Product Name
- Current Year's Revenue
- Current Year's Gross Margin
- Current Year's Gross Margin %
- Current Year's Quantity Sold
- Customer Type
- Market Segment
- Sales Office
- Primary Plant
- Material Type

The transaction file is typically quite large; consequently, we only look at the most recent 12 months. However, if you notice a major shift from the other files then you will want to go back and capture this data.

The final worksheet needed is purchases from vendors. The columns of data to extract are:

- Vendor ID

- Vendor Name

- Prior Year Purchases – Dollars Invoiced

- Prior Year Quantity Purchased

- Current Year Purchases – Dollars Invoiced

- Current Year Quantity Purchased

Usually this material comes in raw form. The data will need basic cleanup work such as formatting columns, removing unneeded decimal places and color-coding the worksheet headers. Expect all of these files to be large, especially the transaction file. Our suggestion is to run the extractions, especially of the transaction file, at night to minimize potential disruptions to daily operations of the business.

Gross Margin as Value Surrogate

In the Red Light/Green Light Analysis you will look at several key metrics, but once you push beyond this into your Quad analysis gross margin will be the driving metric. Why choose gross margin as the key analytical metric? What makes this metric a better choice than alternative variables such as revenue, quantity produced, or gross margin percentage?

First let's define Gross Margin and talk briefly about the accounting that drives its calculation. Gross Margin is typically calculated as revenue less direct material costs, direct labor costs, and indirect overhead costs allocated to the product (or customer). Some companies may include freight or some type of customer rebate back into these numbers but these tend to be more the exception than the rule. It is impractical to allocate expenses based on every single transaction in a company. If you are producing a million widgets, you are not going to calculate the actual manufacturing costs of each unique widget. Instead, companies calculate a standard cost, which is the average cost of producing a widget. This standard cost allocates expenses based on certain operating assumptions. Sometimes the outside world changes or the assumptions are incorrect. These anomalies and deviations from expectations are recorded in variance accounts. Ideally, these variances are fairly small as a percentage of the overall cost and inconsequential. However, many companies view their cost accounting System and the allocation of standard costs as somewhat suspect. This issue needs to be addressed, if managers are to support the results of the 80/20 analysis.

If the consensus is that the standards are significantly inaccurate then plan on going back and doing additional analysis work to adjust the results. This is especially critical if variances are running 15% to 20% of the overall cost. Reasonable accuracy is important not only to reaching proper conclusions but also to ensure that these conclusions have management support.

Cost accounting systems tend to be thought of as existing primarily in manufacturing; however, they are just as relevant in service industries. All companies need to know the cost of producing and/or providing their products and services. If a special froth, nutmeg latte takes three more minutes to prepare than to pour a cup of coffee, then the price of that latte better reflect this fact. We are confident that Starbucks knows exactly how long it takes to make their lattes and the general cost of the ingredients. They also need to have a system for allocating indirect overhead to their products.

As we dive into the Quad Analysis, many of your decisions will be based on the data gathered through your accounting process. You should perform at least a spot check to provide some comfort level as to the accuracy of the information. This is not a barrier to moving forward, it is just good due diligence. Getting cross-functional acceptance that the data is accurate will help mitigate criticisms later that the analysis was based on questionable cost accounting data. This type of objection may occur when you propose eliminating someone's favorite project that hasn't gone anywhere in several years. The key is to surface these objections early in the process before they become a barrier to progress.

As in any sampling process, you should make certain that your choices are representative of the population as a whole. You want to use a random process to pick them within their sub-categories but also review your choices to make certain you have sufficiently spread them over your population. Make certain you are using good sampling practices. Sort of like sampling a box of chocolates—don't pick them all from the exact same corner of the box otherwise you might think the entire box is coconut crème filled.

This sampling involves taking some products or services and tracking their expenses. Is the time allocated to make the product correct? When you add up the raw material does it truly add up to the expense of the products? When you look at your customers are there major cost differences in your after-production delivery of the goods and services? We are looking for variances beyond the 15% to 20%. You can look at the labor, material, and scrap variance accounts buried within your income statement to see percentages and go forth from there.

Even if variances are significant, the analysis work is relative. As long as everything is right or wrong in the same direction then you are fine to use the numbers. Typically when we dig into the data we find they are more accurate than perceived. In practice the gross margin numbers and the results from the analysis produce good results. We have never had an analysis derailed because of faulty gross margin numbers, but we have had people question the gross margin numbers after an analysis was complete. It can be particularly helpful to be able to pull in the accounting department and have them explain that we did the sampling and the numbers seemed reasonably correct when there is push back from a team member losing their favorite non-performing project.

Why do we examine gross margin rather than revenue? Gross margin is critical because this best represents where the value exists within an organization. One might try to argue that revenue is a better focus since it has more potential if properly streamlined. However, revenue doesn't pay your salary and it definitely doesn't indicate the relative value the market places on your products. Are you more concerned with making revenue numbers or making a larger paycheck?

You wouldn't want to focus your business around a high revenue generator that provides no profit. Focusing on high running SKU's would just be inherently wrong. While there will be some type of correlation between what you make a lot of and your gross margin, using this as a driving metric to guide focus and resource allocation would be misguided. It would be like picking people to play basketball strictly based on their height. **Gross Margin is your surrogate for value**. This approach presumes an efficient market—a market that pays for what it values. It presumes that management is smart enough to price the product properly. Remember, one of us went to the University of Chicago. Businesses where gross margin isn't relevant are rare, but they do exist—software, for example.

Clustering Customers And Products

Often in the data scrubbing process you need to make decisions about the grouping of products and/or customers. Is a product packaged in different quantities one item or multiple? Should you group private label items along with your standard product offering? How do you lump your customers? Is it by ship-to addresses or by regional buying hubs, for example?

As an example, suppose you work for Nabisco (today a division of Mondelez International—formerly Kraft). You'd like to know how many Oreos you sold last quarter. An innocent question and seemingly simple to answer. Over 450 billion Oreos have been sold since their debut in 1912.[9] As for how many were sold last quarter, it depends.

Start with recipes. At the very least Mondelez is likely to have a standard recipe and a kosher recipe (they do business in Israel). What of other recipe variations; perhaps substituting high fructose corn syrup for sugar? Do we add up all the variations of recipe or do we keep track by recipe?

How about packaging variations? Oreos are packaged in the classic three-column package, in packages of six, and of two. They are bundled as part of Lunchables meals. Most likely, other variations exist. Do we count the number of packages and multiply by the appropriate number of Oreos per package? Is there some system where we can count the number of Oreos we produced before they went into packages? If we can manage to count how many Oreos we made, how does that map to how many we manage to sell?

That may get us through standard Oreos. How do we count the Oreos with orange-colored centers sold at Halloween in the US? Green-colored Oreos sold for St. Patrick's Day? Double Stuf Oreos? Double Stuf Oreos with orange-colored centers? Mini-bite-size Snak-Paks? Mondelez identifies 46 different versions of the Oreo on their Web site and doesn't appear to count Oreos packaged within another product (the Lunchables question).

That covers most of the relevant business reasons that make counting Oreos tricky. There are likely additional, technical reasons that will make the problem harder, not easier. The various systems that track production, distribution, and sales have likely been implemented at different times and may have slight variations in how and when they count things. Those differences need to be identified and then reconciled. Someone will have to discover and reconcile the different codes and identifiers used to identify Oreos in each discrete system. And so on. Fortunately, Oreos are an extreme example. In practice, grouping products or customers is a more straightforward task.

What should generally drive the choice is what best represents economic reality rather than accounting convenience. If a product manufacturing process is identical except for a packaging label applied at the end, then you would probably lump those products together. If a customer's distribution center makes no purchasing decisions and is just a ship to address then you would probably combine the distribution center data with the purchasing office location's data as a single customer. To make these decisions properly you need people who know the production process and the customer base. They need to review the data and approve the clustering decisions. Depending on the number of SKUs, this process usually takes one or two days. However, you are already starting to analyze the data and its messages.

Red Light/Green Light Analysis (80/20 Data Manipulation)

A red light/green light analysis starts the team's data analysis. You now have worksheets with customer data and product data and are in a position to discover whether the 80/20 rule holds for your organization. Typically the break points are near 80 and 20. On occasion, as little as ten percent of products or customers account for ninety percent of gross margin. We have yet to encounter a situation where the data did not conform to an 80/20 type of distribution. Use a cross functional team to work through the data: General Manager, Sales, Operations, Engineering, Purchasing, and Accounting. You can also have different people with specialized knowledge come and go during the process.

Usually management already knows most of the information revealed in a red light/green light analysis, so it is important that you set reasonable expectations as you go into this part of the process. Even though the information is already known – you will want to still go through it in detail. Expect it to take a day or two. Occasionally you will find some interesting insight, but for the most part you will reconfirm prior understandings. If you do find something truly insightful this is a bonus.

You are accomplishing three key things when you take your company through the red light/green light analysis:

1.   Building your team and bringing them on board with a data driven process.

2.   Going through the numbers and double-checking the figures before you do the more complicated Quad Analysis.

3.   Grounding the team in the data.

The worksheet data contains a cross section of information. During the red light/green light portion of this process you will focus on a variety of columns: revenue, gross margin percent and inventory, but your Quad analysis will be done using strictly the gross margin number. Finally, to provide additional clarity to your business you will divide gross margin percent into a high, middle, and low range to better understand pertinent trends or patterns.

As shown on the previous examples (Exhibit 3) the revenue, gross margin, and margin percentages are color coded to enhance comprehension and make the process more visual. The following pages sketch the mechanics of manipulating the worksheets from the data dump to generate the 80/20 data. Appendix 2 examines these mechanics in more detail for those who prefer more depth.

Data in the revenue, gross margin, and gross margin percent columns drives the 80/20 assessment and the consequent color-coding. Start with the revenue column and sort revenue from highest to lowest. Add an additional column to record cumulative revenue and locate the row where the cumulative revenue reaches 80% of total revenue. Set the color of all the rows up to this point green.

An 80/20 purist would color the remaining SKU rows below this line red. We favor a yellow section for the 80-95% range. Three sections yield more insight than two. In addition, three sections mitigate concerns about digging too deep in the product elimination phase that follows. Reviewing the potential elimination of 5% of your gross margin is much more palatable than discussing the potential elimination of the 20%. Most people at this stage in the process can't get past this concept so making it a less threatening number helps. Starting the process of eliminating low-value items is challenging. Once this process starts it takes on a life of its own. An initial focus on the items that collectively account for the last 5% is something that few resist.

Every organization we have ever reviewed has sufficient excess SKU's/Customers in this 5% range. Often this is when you will get the "WOW" effect by illustrating the number of SKU's or customers below this 5% level. This tends to make a compelling argument about the potential impact of the simplification process and people become more enthusiastic.

You leave this color code in place and then re-sort the data based on the gross margin, adding the accumulation column and doing the exact same color-coding process.

At this point you can see the group of your products/customers by their revenue and gross margin color coded by their respective 80/20 ranking within the organization. This provides some minor insight into the relationship between revenue ranking and gross margin ranking. Spreadsheets with a long tail (i.e. more 80/20 SKU's and/or customers with gross margin than revenue) tend to tell you that you may be heavily discounting your large revenue products to supplement volume.

Next you go to your gross margin percent and highlight some of this column looking for patterns. You should sort your red light/green light file based on gross margin percentage. Historically for manufacturing companies we have used the following rule to sort a product mix 50% or higher is highlighted in green, 35% to 50% is highlighted in yellow, and any SKU or Customer below 35% is highlighted in red. In our experience, for a manufacturing business, 50% tends to be the required cross over point to have a long-term, viable business.

For a distribution business you would typically have a slightly lower gross margin percent. 30% and above could be highlighted green, 20% to 30% could be highlighted yellow, and below 20% could be highlighted red. There aren't any real hard and fast rules in the choosing of the percentages. The intent here is to sort your business into high, middle, and low gross margin percentages. Divide the data into thirds.

Make certain to do a thorough job vetting the data. Once you get into the Quad Analysis the process is more technical and challenging in terms of building a consensus around the impact of the data. Build an early consensus that the data is correct. If by chance you didn't get accurate gross margin, you can always circle back and redo this process. However, it is anti-climatic to build your Quads and then conclude that gross margin should have included rebates to customers or that information from your cost accounting system is suspect and have to revisit this section of the analysis.

Finally, when you develop the 80/20 tables you should include what we call the crossover threshold. It is that point where you go from one classification (80/20) to the other (20/80). It is used especially when you start to look at new products and decide if you should add or eliminate a product. It can also be viewed as the point where a customer or product will switch from one Quad to another Quad.

Even with color-coding, the spreadsheets depicted in Exhibit 3 can be overwhelming in their detail, making it difficult to extract insights. It is helpful to summarize the mass of detail into a single set of totals for each category. What can we learn from looking at this summary level for customers, products, and vendors?

Exhibit 4
Example Of A Red Light/Green Light Summary—Customers

	Revenue	Number	Percent	Crossover Threshold
80/20	12,000,000	25	6.25%	1,525,000
95/05	3,500,000	50	12.50%	85,000
05/95	2,000,000	325	81.25%	0
Total	14,000,000	400	100.00%	

	Gross Margin	Number	Percent	Crossover Threshold
80/20	1,750,000	37	9.25%	62,500
95/05	345,000	65	16.25%	13,750
05/95	235,000	298	74.50%	0
Total	1,985,000	400	100.00%	

80/20	14.58%
95/05	9.86%
05/95	11.75%
Total	14.18%

The customer analysis reveals the following:

- 25 customers, or 6.25%of the total customer base, generate 80% of the revenue.

- 75 customers account for 95% of total revenue.

- 325 customers account for the remaining 5% of revenue.

- On the gross margin side of the ledger:

- 37 customers account for 80% of the total gross margin.

- 102 customers account for 95% of gross margin.

- 298 customers contribute the remaining 5% of total gross margin in the company.

- The 80/20 Crossover Threshold is $85,000 in revenue and $13,750 in gross margin.

Exhibit 5
Example Of A Red Light/Green Light Summary—Products

	Revenue	Number	Percent	Crossover Threshold
80/20	12,750,000	60	4.14%	17,800,000
95/05	325,000	125	8.62%	125,000
05/95	1,250,000	1265	87.24%	0
Total	14,000,000	1450	100.00%	

	Gross Margin	Number	Percent	Crossover Threshold
80/20	1,235,000	28	1.93%	67,000
95/05	230,000	137	9.45%	12,500
05/95	750,000	1285	88.62%	0
Total	1,985,000	1450	100.00%	

80/20	9.69%
95/05	70.77%
05/95	60.00%
Total	14.18%

The product analysis reveals the following:

- 60 products, or 4.14% of the overall catalog, account for 80% of revenue.

- 185 products account for 95% of total revenue.

- 1265 products, or 87.24%, constitute the remaining 5%.

On the gross margin side of the ledger:

- 28 products, or 1.93% of the product, make up 80% of gross margin.

- 137 products bring the company to the 95% mark.

- 1285 products produce only 5% of total gross margin and perform at a much lower gross margin percentage.

- The product revenue 80/20 crossover threshold is $125,000 and gross margin threshold is $12,500.

Exhibit 6
Example Of A Red Light/Green Light Summary—Vendors

	Purchases	Quantity	Percent	Crossover Threshold
80/20	6,250,000	45	11.11%	47500
95/05	635000	60	14.81%	8700
05/95	137000	300	74.07%	0
Total	7,022,000	405		

The vendor analysis reveals:

- 45 core vendors accounting for 80% of purchases.

- 60 additional suppliers bringing the total to 95% of purchases.

- 300 remaining vendors that tend to be ancillary in nature; sometimes they are critical, but most often they are extraneous to the overall functioning of the business.

These types of ratios are typical of the companies we have reviewed. A handful of core customers and products drive the overall business. Multiple secondary products and small customers create significant complexity without corresponding value. The 80/20 rule always holds and more often than not the distribution is skewed closer to 90/10.

Does this company fit the 80/20 rule? Absolutely.

In practice, we find it useful to organize these summary tables into a single exhibit. This table (Exhibit 7) provides a snapshot of the organization that highlights the interaction between customers and products.

Exhibit 7
Example Of A Red Light/Green Light Summary—Vendors

CUSTOMERS

	Revenue	Number	Percent	Crossover Threshold
80/20	12,000,000	25	6.25%	1,525,000
95/05	3,500,000	50	12.50%	85,000
05/95	2,000,000	325	81.25%	0
Total	14,000,000	400	100.00%	

	Gross Margin	Number	Percent	Crossover Threshold
80/20	1,750,000	37	9.25%	62,500
95/05	345,000	65	16.25%	13,750
05/95	235,000	298	74.50%	0
Total	1,985,000	400	100.00%	

80/20	14.58%
95/05	9.86%
05/95	11.75%
Total	14.18%

PRODUCTS

	Revenue	Number	Percent	Crossover Threshold
80/20	12,750,000	60	4.14%	17,800,000
95/05	325,000	125	8.62%	125,000
05/95	1,250,000	1265	87.24%	0
Total	14,000,000	1450	100.00%	

	Gross Margin	Number	Percent	Crossover Threshold
80/20	2,235,000	28	1.93%	67,000
95/05	230,000	137	9.45%	12,500
05/95	250,000	1285	83.62%	0
Total	1,985,000	1450	100.00%	

80/20	9.69%
95/05	70.77%
05/95	60.00%
Total	14.18%

VENDORS

	Purchases	Quantity	Percent	Crossover Threshold
80/20	6,250,000	45	11.11%	47500
95/05	635000	60	14.81%	8700
05/95	137000	300	74.0%	0
Total	7,022,000	405		

Some reasons that so many products and customers exist are due to legacy where one customer wanted something one way while another customer wanted something another way. The SKU or Customer still might exist there and thus the product offering was increased. Companies appear inherently open to adding complexity to an organization. A customer inquiry will come in with a seemingly minor change, the engineering team will say they can get it done, and then in comes the order and complexity rises. Often, there is no systemic vetting process of minor variations in product or customers. Often, upper management is most complicit in unintended growth in complexity.

When you look at these numbers the initial reaction is to think that the easiest solution is to simply eliminate the bottom 5%. Some business executives have come to believe that 80/20 is strictly a product elimination process of carving out the lower non-performing part of your business. Problem solved? Companies that do this tend to end up in a lot of trouble.

Why wouldn't you want to simply eliminate 5% or 20% products that are creating the complexity?

- Maybe a 20/80 product is key to serving your largest customer.

- Maybe a 20/80 product is keeping one of your competitors out of a segment.

- Maybe a 20/80 product is your next up and coming high growth product.

You need to understand the data.

You have new information that provides basic insight into the organization. You have gone through the details and come to some consensus amongst your team members about the data spread based on an 80/20 filter.

The red light/green light process is not about finding major insight into your data. Chances are you already know your top customers and products. What is critical in this process is scrubbing the data and involving a cross functional team in the review process. You are also building involvement, commitment and support across the organization as you go to the next step: the Quad Analysis.

CHAPTER 5
QUAD ANALYSIS–REASSEMBLING THE NUMBERS

After using the 80/20 analysis to rank customers and products, you enter the process we call Quad Analysis. As suggested, this analysis breaks into four pieces, or four "boxes of insight."

The 80/20 analysis just completed helps focus on an organization's most important customers or its most important products. In itself, however, it does nothing to address the perennial problem of organizational silos. The Quad Map explicitly integrates the customer and product perspectives. As Exhibit 8 illustrates, we push the 80/20 analysis a step farther by examining the intersection of customer and product data.

Exhibit 8
Bringing Customer and Product Results Together

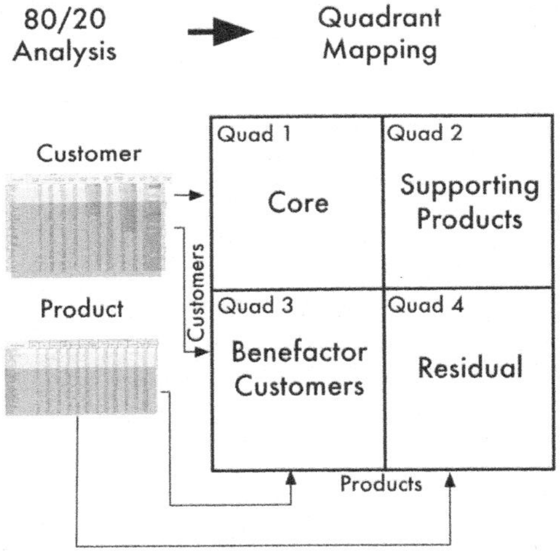

The 2x2 matrix is a frequent source of ridicule by operating managers toward outside analysts and consultants. Perhaps they have a hazy memory of similar diagrams from some introductory strategy class in business school. In the 1970s, the Boston Consulting Group created strategy consulting as a distinct segment in the management services industry. BCG's signature analysis was to evaluate a client's product portfolio in terms of market share and growth rates. They presented the analysis in the form of another 2x2 matrix known as the Growth/Share Matrix. BCG's analysis focused on questions about strategy, while the Quad analysis focuses on questions about operations and markets.

The 2x2 display format often smells of naiveté and oversimplification to those on the production floor or in the sales offices. Some managers will dismiss this process as not relevant in their organization. They feel that their company is too complex, order demand is too unpredictable, or that this particular method doesn't apply to their business.

The germ of truth buried in this skepticism is that this particular 2x2 matrix, the "Quad Map", is the last piece of analysis that can be done in the back office. It has not been vetted against the reality of day-to-day operations. It is an intentional simplification of the otherwise overwhelming cacophony of customers, products, and their internal advocates vying for the resources of the organization. It creates an intermediate lens into the business that hides details of each individual product or customer to reveal larger patterns that can be exploited.

Why four Quads? Any business is a complex matrix of customers and products. Each Quad represents a discrete classification of customers and products. With its own set of objectives and tools to use in dealing with various situations. These objectives and tools are similar regardless of the products and customers.

If you look only at products you get a distorted sense of value of what your key customers are purchasing from you. Customers generally purchase a basket of goods to fulfill a variety of needs across of given niche. If you don't offer enough of an array of products to meet your customers' needs you open the door for a competitor to take the business, or you leave opportunity unfilled for both yourself in terms of lost revenue or your customer in terms of their needs.

If you look solely at key customers you get some understanding of the market dynamics driving the business. You also want to grasp aspects of market concentration and sorting your customers as to what is driving their placement within the quads. We want to see the ordering patterns of different customers especially if there is a difference between Quad 1 and Quad 3. Then you look deeper to see if the ordering pattern that exists within certain customers and products represents a deeper pattern.

There is tremendous strength when you bring these two perspectives together to understand your business. How you set up your systems and flow through the business is going to depend on the interaction of these two.

Reassembling the Numbers

Exhibit 9 depicts how the numbers from a hypothetical 80/20 analysis map onto Quads.

Exhibit 9
A Hypothetical Quad Analysis

	Quad 1	**Quad 2**	
20/80 (Top 20% customers ~80% of Margin)	Customers: 75 Products: 20 Sales: $12.8M Margin: $ 5.8M	Customers: 59 Products: 35 Sales: $ 3.8M Margin: $ 1.4M	**79%** of Total Margin
	Quad 3	**Quad 4**	
80/20 (Remaining 80% ~20% of Margin)	Customers: 425 Products: 19 Sales: $ 3.2M Margin: $ 1.3M	Customers: 525 Products: 44 Sales: $ 1.5M Margin: $ 0.5M	**21%** of Total Margin

(Left axis: **Customers**)

Products

20/80 (Top 20% SKUs ~80% of Margin)	80/20 (Remaining 80% ~20% of Margin)
78% of Total Margin	22% of Total Margin

The Quad Analysis is developed from the 80/20 analysis of gross margins in the business. The mechanics of generating the initial Quad map are discussed in detail in Appendix 2.

Any competent spreadsheet user can follow those instructions to generate the Quad Map so the exact mechanics can usually be left up to a computer savvy accountant. The mechanical process assigns customer/product transactions to a Quad based on the crossover thresholds set during the Red Light/Green Light analysis. With these evidence-based assignments complete, the next step is to adjust the assignments to factor in the organization's contextual knowledge of existing operations, sales, and distribution activities.

The mass of numbers that Exhibit 9 organizes and summarizes may not immediately convey the "news" it represents. A cursory examination might suggest that this exercise has done nothing more than divide the business into four distinct pieces. If you scale the quadrants such that the area of each quadrant represents the corresponding percentage of the whole, the message becomes more evident. Exhibit 10 portrays the analysis from a gross margin perspective.

Exhibit 10
Quadrants Scaled by Gross Margin

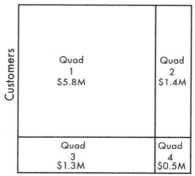

Products

The combination of customers and products falling into Quad 1 represent significantly more than half of the organization's total gross margin. While compelling in its own right, examining Quad 1 from the simple perspective of the number of customers and products that constitute the Quad amplifies the point even further. Exhibit 11 portrays the Quadrants in proportion to the number of customers and products in each Quadrant as a percentage of the whole. The sum of the number of customers and products assigned to each Quad provides a simple proxy of managerial complexity.

Exhibit 11
Quadrants Scaled by Customer/Product Count

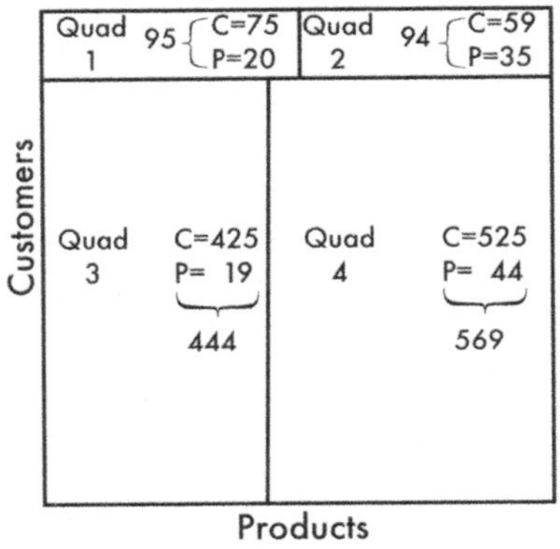

Quad 1	95 { C=75 P=20	Quad 2	94 { C=59 P=35	
Quad 3	C=425 P= 19 444	Quad 4	C=525 P= 44 569	

(Customers — vertical axis; Products — horizontal axis)

Improvement opportunities exist in the asymmetry of these two distributions. Every business has a core—a small group of customers and products—that accounts for most of the economic value. The reality is that most businesses allocate the same managerial skills, focus, and attention to each Quad when those scarce resources can be better distributed.

Starting the Journey with Quad Map in Hand

We've referred to the Quad Map as a treasure map. As with any map, the map is not the territory itself. We must take the map out of the conference room and into the day-to-day operations of the organization. Recall Exhibit 10 and 11 from the preceding section. They presented two perspectives on the existing business; one economic, the other complexity. Place them side-by-side, as in Exhibit 12, and they suggest how different the management challenges actually are across the organization.

Exhibit 12
Quadrants from Economic and Complexity Perspectives

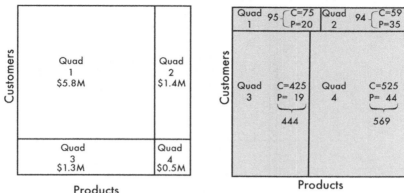

Quad 1 and Quad 4 are out of balance, even if we can't yet explain what might account for balance or imbalance. In Quad 1, a small portion of your business in terms of customers and products accounts for most of your economic success. At the opposite extreme, in Quad 4, substantial portions of your customer base and product line contribute little to your organization's economic health. Quads 2 and 3 appear more balanced in terms of their complexity relative to their economic contributions to the organization.

An alternate way to view the Quadrants is to ask how much gross margin the organization generates per item to be managed in each Quad. In Quad 1, selling 20 products to 75 customers generates $5.8 million dollars of gross margin. At the other extreme, in Quad 4, selling 44 products to 525 customers generates only $500,000 in gross margin. Exhibit 13 condenses these relationships into a gross margin per unit of complexity.

Exhibit 13
Gross Margin per Unit of Complexity

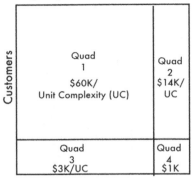

Products

While the calculation may be crude, it reinforces that each Quad presents distinct management challenges.

Understanding The Quads

Exhibit 14
Quad 1—Core

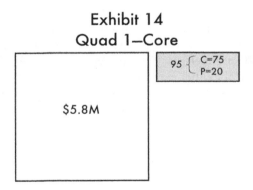

The value of your business is anchored in Quad 1. This combination of your most profitable customers' purchases and your most profitable products typically contributes more to your success than all of the remaining Quads. Everything you do should be centered on the efficient and effective manufacturing and servicing of your products and customers in Quad 1.

Businesses tend to use the language of optimization loosely. We seek "best practices. " We speak of "optimizing" inventories or plant floors.

Quality levels should exceed six sigma or other desired levels of performance. This talk obscures two realities; one about our decision capabilities, one about the parts vs. the whole.

Economist Herbert Simon[10] won the Nobel Prize for inventing the notion of "bounded rationality" to account for how organizations manage to make good enough decisions in the real world in spite of our cognitive limitations. Decision makers do not have to be omniscient or perfectly rational; they need only pursue decisions that prove good enough. For all the talk of optimization in boardrooms or C-suites, performing "better than the competition" will generally carry the day. In Simon's terms we "satisfice" rather than optimize. Given those cognitive limits, anything that focuses attention and limits the factors that need to be evaluated helps.

The second, and more important, reality is that organizations are complex systems. Effective complex systems must trade off performance among subsystems for the system as a whole to perform at a sufficiently high level. If you tune each component of an enterprise to perform as well as each possibly can, the system will perform less well overall. An organization, for example, that has tuned its production processes to minimize work-in-process inventory, minimize production set up costs, and maximize output cannot respond to special orders as quickly as a custom job shop with lots of raw materials and spare capacity.

In organizations that do not seek a way to see the enterprise as an integral system, tradeoff decisions are based less on the available data and more on the power and influence that individual functions, subsystems, and managers have accumulated over time. Much of the time, the results may, in fact, be satisfactory. But, at best, these decisions can only be locally satisfactory. Again, Quad 1 provides a data-driven lens to examine these tradeoff opportunities.

What are these opportunities? Which bread, meat, and milk do you plan on keeping in the refrigerator over the long-term? These choices are going to determine your long-term health. You wouldn't want to stock a lot of baloney when everyone in family prefers roast beef.

We are not suggesting that you stay static as an organization and focus solely on what you currently do well. However, it is essential to understand your existing core competencies while focusing your business around these so you can make the proper strategic decisions going forward to amplify the growth in gross margin and value.

As you look at the list of customers and products that constitute your Quad 1 you want to understand: Are the products being sold through the same distribution channels? How are customers spread out geographically?

Do you have different segments that exist within Quad 1? Are some customers purchasing one set of products and another customer purchasing a different set of products? Are these products that are made to stock or made to order? Do they use the same manufacturing assets and processes? Is there a technological difference to them?

In one recent business review the Quad Analysis revealed two distinct types of products and customers in Quad 1. All were being served by the same company, using the same processes. Some of the products had crossover and a lot of the same components were used in product sold into each market so this blurred the data sufficiently to camouflage the actual situation.

The growth in each channel had occurred organically so the organization had just gotten used to managing through it. Everyone suspected this existed, but no one had called it out and the data quickly brought it to light.

When the businesses were separated it was found that the OEM defined portion of the business had high predictable demand cadence, large volume and consistent product mix. The distributor side of the business had a tremendous amount of complexity and required the ability to quickly change over equipment and create down-stream subassemblies that could be easily brought together on short notice. This required a different set of manufacturing practices than the OEM group. This two-market reality wasn't apparent until the company started peeling away the Quad 1 customers and categorizing them.

Before we identified this opportunity the company had unsuccessfully tried to run all of the products through the same manufacturing process in the same fashion resulting in back orders, frequent stock outs and expensive break-ins. Not that either the OEM or the Distribution business is good or bad. It is just that each segment required a different set of manufacturing techniques. By focusing on each one individually we were able to bring the necessary processes in place to improve the gross margin in the OEM business and simplify the complexity inherent in the distributor business. This resulted in a significant increase in operating income and a general simplification of the business.

One of the things you want to do is to review the flow of products through the plant or delivery platform for services as if Quad 1 was the entire business. How could you organize your facility and platform to make the flow more seamless? One of the key steps is to start by stripping out non-value added work. Figure out what you would need to do by examining your toolkit for ways you can maximize your value and eliminate complexity. This process is the heart of Part 2. However, the first step in this process is defining what you do best. What are your pre-existing constraints and opportunities? What would these look like if they were stand-alone operations without all of complexity of the other Quads? We always find a small, manageable sub-set of the customers and products in this Quad.

In answering these questions you will begin to develop a coherent understanding of your Quad 1. The key here is that none of the answers are the same amongst organizations. The answers are always different but the process is the same and the triggers that you use from your toolkit will be the same. Which ones you focus on will depend upon the information/landscape you find in your specific mix of products, customers, and industry. Truly understanding your Quad 1 from raw material to collection is exceptionally informative.

Strategy is about defining the core business in terms of ideas such as sustainable competitive advantage, barriers to entry and power relative to buyers and suppliers. Starting from a clean sheet of paper with just your Quad 1, allows you to best define key products/services and customers where value of what you offer is most appreciated by the market.

Much of the work of strategy consulting firms lies in teasing out insights about core products, markets and economics that are obscured in the accounting and operational systems of the average organization.

Quad 1 analysis grounds these questions in the facts and performance of the current organization's best customers and best products. Quad 1 represents the strong core of the current business. Without getting this right it is difficult to move on to any other part of the business.

Exhibit 15
Quad 2—Supporting Products

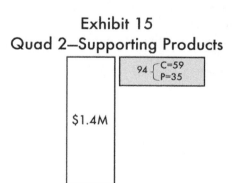

Quad 2 products exist only to support the Quad 1 customers. By definition these products exist to maintain your Quad 1 customers and, thus, customers here are a subset of the Quad 1 customers. During the application of the toolkit, you will develop an understanding of why these products exist. What market need are they servicing? You might sell a Quad 2 product to a Quad 3 customer, but your reason to keep the product in the catalog will be based on your Quad 1 customers.

Sometimes these are just products that are classed incorrectly and should technically be a Quad 1 except for some minor variation that has caused them to have a different SKU number. If this is the case, and the manufacturing and/or service platform is identical in nature then you should consolidate them.

For Quad 2 – think of something like milk at McDonalds. Not necessarily what pays the overhead, but critical to some of your key patrons. In time, some of your Quad 2 can grow into your Quad 1. When McDonalds first offered salads, they could be seen as a Quad 2 offering. Today, they have matured into a Quad 1 product of their own.

Questions you want to ask about your Quad 2: How do these products fit into the overall mix of your Quad 1 products? Are there product offerings you can consolidate or move from Quad 2 to Quad 1? How do these complicate your manufacturing/service component? Do customers really care if the product is "Royal Blue" rather than "Ocean Blue" or was this just an isolated request that got slipped into your product offering and then grew a few more customers because it was available? What happens if you offer the product only in an "Ocean Blue" style?

You also want to understand the depth of your Quad 2 products. Is it sold to only one or two Quad 1 customers or does the Quad 2 product have a wider following? Why do some customers purchase a Quad 2 product but others might not? Are we missing opportunities or creating complexity? Not so much to just eliminate them, but because we want to understand the interference so we can properly manage it. In the Toolkit section of the book you will find recommended techniques for managing the Quad 2.

Exhibit 16
Quad 3—Benefactor Customers

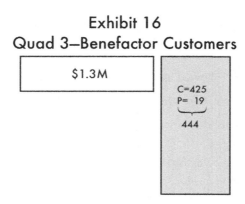

These customers exist because they are purchasing the Quad 1 product mix and consequently are easy to service. Make certain that this is the case. In theory, you already have the product in stock or the organization as a whole is already geared up to manufacture or service. Incremental transaction costs should be minimal.

Think about the patron who just stops at Starbucks once a week on the trip back from yoga class. The infrastructure is in place to service this person and the cost of providing that service is inconsequential, although it would be impossible to keep the store running if you serviced only sporadic monthly customers. Companies recognize this by using frequent visitor coupons so that you actually get a free item after your 10th visit.

Quad 3 customers do not have the buying volume you would need to sustain the business. However, they can still be an important element to overall profitability. Sometimes there will be a synergistic, competitive relationship between the Quad 1 and Quad 3 customers such as adjacent distribution channels. These are channels where you might find other products that you can manufacture and sell but only if over time they could grow into a Quad 1 product.

While performing an analysis for one business we found that we typically had a single Quad 1 customer (distributor) in each major city and then 3-4 Quad 3 customers (distributors) as well. This led to an insightful discussion about the marketing approach and strategy of the company overall. As we dug into the Quad classifications we found that Quad 1 customers purchased all of their products from the company, while Quad 3 Customers in the same geographic territory were cherry picking the line of products.

When we dug deeper we found that the Quad 3 customers tended to be purchasing their core products from an inexpensive competitor that only provided a very narrow offering. In some ways the company was actually supporting its competition by allowing them to stay focused on a very narrow part of the market that didn't require much expertise to manufacture.

The discussion followed as to how best to deal with this situation:

- Do we cut off these Quad 3 customers?

- Do we raise the prices of these Quad 3 customers on select products?

- Do we require customers to sign distribution agreements or bundle items so that Quad 3 customers must purchase a certain amount of all Quad 1 products?

- Do we just leave things as is?

How might the competitor respond? There isn't any one right answer since it depends on the industry itself and the economics – the important point is that the data analysis highlighted this situation. It wasn't understood at the upper management level until we looked first at the customers, then at their product purchases. We discovered that a lot of the Quad 3 customers were purchasing only a small subset of Quad 1 and Quad 2 products relative to the product catalog as a whole. The perception had been that these were just smaller customers. In actuality there was a lot of selective purchasing going on. During the discussions, it was interesting to see the sales manager quickly figure out who their primary competitor was for most of the Quad 3's companies. He claimed that he had sensed what was going on, but it wasn't until the data analysis was complete that the evidence confirmed his instincts.

In this case the organization elected to figure out a way to raise prices to these Quad 3 companies that were selectively purchasing. That being said there is no correct answer—it is about understanding the data, the markets, and the industry so you can make the correct strategic choice.

Not all Quad 3 customers are just cherry picking. Quad 3 customers can play a critical role for your organization. You just want to have a clear strategy to manage them. You want to think through your sales and marketing strategy to meet Quad 3 customer needs in a way that doesn't interfere with Quad 1. Quad 1 customers are the Crown Jewels—they drive your business. When you set-up your business model you want to arrange items around your Quad 1. Since Quad 3 customers typically purchase in smaller quantities their transaction costs are relatively higher than Quad 1 customers even if they happen to be low on an absolute basis. You want to make certain you charge them accordingly.

Exhibit 17
Quad 4—Residual

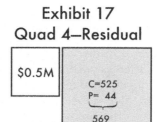

Products and customers in Quad 4 tend to be entities that add unnecessary complexity to your company or occasionally conceal hidden gems (but mostly complexity). Often they fit into the following categories:

- Products that were introduced several years back and never succeeded.

- Products that no one had the inclination or time to eliminate.

- New products or customers that need time to develop.

- Parts for prior models where the company lacks a defined obsolescence process.

- Smaller, one off customers with special needs.

The initial reaction of folks is that you immediately come in and eliminate Quad 4 Products and Customers, but this is not the case. You need to thoroughly review each one and come to a proper decision for the business.

Every business is different. You have to be very systematic and deliberate when you review why you are manufacturing product or keeping a customer in Quad 4. If you do decide to eliminate products or customers, it all doesn't have to be done at one time. You can also eliminate items in stages so it is less problematic for the organization as whole.

However, these represent enormous opportunities to simplify a company with little or no impact on the gross margin. Do not be enticed by the high margin siren song. Just because something has a high margin doesn't mean you should keep it. It is also adding complexity and noise to your business and is obscuring your ability to see other possibilities that exist for your Quad 1. You need to eliminate it if it doesn't have major potential to turn into a Quad 1 product. Selling a lot of Quad 4 products is not a sustainable business strategy. It takes a while to fully appreciate this.

Some items will be obvious candidates for elimination. Other products/customers will offer opportunities for new ideas to grow and develop. The key to thoroughly vetting a Quad 4 item is to have a cross functional team participate. You want to truly understand the complexity that is being introduced into the business. If you have a product and/or customer that is forcing you to do something outside of your Quad 1 Products (your core competency)—you want to challenge yourself as to why you are in this product, service, or customer.

For example, consider a community hospital deciding to offer yoga classes. Would you think of going to a hospital for yoga classes? While hospitals and yoga are both about health, providing instructional classes on exercise isn't generally among a hospital's core competences. Yoga classes may appear to be a reasonable service line extension, yet ultimately prove to be a Quad 4 service whose complexity outweighs its economic contribution. This thought process applies to examining product mix across Quad 4.

The other key process is how you manage the elimination of Quad 4 items. There are several techniques available. Simply telling customers that products are no longer available or that you don't want to sell to a particular customer tends to have negative consequences. The process needs to be managed. Suggestions on how to eliminate your Quad 4 are discussed in the following section.

Finally you want to see if there are any holes in your system for the development of more Quad 4 products. Understand who has the responsibility and authority to set-up new SKU's. Often things slip in because of a customer request, operations says "yes", and before you know it a new SKU has been created. Having one or more speed bumps to change can add tremendous value to a company. Just learning to say "No" can be very difficult for some organizations.

Quad Analysis as a Path to Insight

Quad Analysis doesn't create change in an organization. It's a systematic, data driven methodology to organize and examine the evidence contained within your organization's existing information systems. The analysis provides exceptional insight to the most promising areas for improvement and highlights non-contributing complexity. There are different manufacturing processes that are appropriate to the differing situations represented by each Quad.

Despite the emphasis on looking at the data and on the power of 80/20 thinking, Quad Analysis is not a simple mechanical exercise. Exactly where to draw the lines between each Quad is an exercise in managerial judgment. How and where you categorize a particular customer/product combination has major implications for what will happen next.

The Quad Analysis is the transition point from the abstract to the concrete. You want to assemble a cross-functional team to carry out this review. The team should start with the general manager, and include someone from each core function: sales, operations, engineering, purchasing, and accounting. They should also be people who can understand the systems of the company as a whole. The dynamics of this team are critical. You are looking for individuals who are willing to not only accept the implications of the analysis, but also willing to translate them into concrete changes in the operations of the business. These people will become your key champions.

You may have people from each function come and go on the team in order to bring in certain expertise. In several cases as you drill down into a specific area you might have someone come in and out of the group or more importantly walk the group out to the area dealing with the specific issue. If you are looking at a core SKU, then you want to understand the process used to manufacture it and best way to do this is to go look at the process from start to finish. You will find interesting information.

You are looking for patterns. Often these can be easy to find. Usually they are commonly known within the organization. More importantly you are looking for processes, raw materials, equipment and customers that are not allowing you to create more coherent themes. You are looking at why things add complexity rather than looking at what makes them simple. You are searching for the outliers that are obscuring your view of delivery, manufacturing, or service platforms.

Don't allow preconceived notions to cause you to dismiss solutions. Look at the data as objectively as possible. Let the data and the analysis lead you in the correct direction.

When you run into an obstacle that is disrupting a pattern–figure out how to work through it and create your pattern. Don't let "we tried that before" get in your way.

This can be very time consuming process. It is probably the most grueling part of the analysis. However, the grounding in the data and collective company knowledge is tremendous. Obviously, you may quickly decide to eliminate some items without discussion but this decision is beneficial in and of itself. This intense grounding in the data from the business will be exceptionally useful when you finally go through your business and start applying your toolkit.

Don't do this exercise primarily by sitting in a conference room. Get out and walk the plant floor, check boxes, look at set ups, ask plant workers about what is difficult to make, look for inventory piles. In one Transformation we had a question about the volume of warehouse space that was being taken up by a product. It was a determining factor in whether we could successfully set-up a Kanban System (See Kanban - Inventory Management Systems). Did we have the physical space to do a specific type of inventory system? The actual volume data of the physical product came into question. We knew what the computer told us, but we decided to double check. So we took our data out to the plant floor, found the product, and walked off the space requirement. It was quick, everyone was involved, and no one could dispute the finding. We found that we had adequate space contrary to the computer reports that everyone had accepted as gospel.

You want to look at your Quads by Product and by Customer and then bring them back together again. And repeat if necessary. Often there is a lot of information to digest. Having a cross functional team allows you to turn and ask – why is this customer important, what makes the manufacturing of this product so difficult, why is this product blue and that one red, is there really a difference between a Sumatra Dry Roast or Malaysian Dark Roast? Do you need extra equipment to make the Sumatra Dry Roast?

Two simple techniques have proven helpful in working through these questions. The first is to take your 80/20 spreadsheets, project them on a conference room wall, and walk through the data line by line. The ability to sort, color code and process information in a spreadsheet is tremendous. The ability to shift and group customers and products quickly and visualize the results make the analysis flow more easily. Remember, you are looking for patterns that exist in the data that you can use later on. The second is to print out sheets of all of the products listing the customers and then all of the customers listing out the products with the provisionally assigned Quad marked next to each one. You can then sort these into piles of various Quads or issues and discuss each one. This may appear a little old school – but it's a very tangible process as you touch and review each piece of paper. This forces a thorough, one at a time review.

In completing the process you are looking to get a clear definition and understanding of your Quads. The first analysis will be driven strictly by the numbers. It is at this point where you apply some management discretion. You may make some intuitive changes to a Quad: combining customers or products to move something out of Quad 2 or Quad 3 into Quad 1. Or decide that some customers that are currently in Quad 3 should be moved into Quad 1 because they are on an upward growth trajectory and you know that within a year they will be much larger. As the project team you should feel comfortable making these types of changes. It is an important part of the process and often missed by people who understand the mechanical side of the process, but miss the criticality of management oversight.

CHAPTER 6
STRENGTHENING THE CORE–
SIMPLIFYING THE PRODUCT LINE

Getting to your fighting weight

Product line simplification is the most powerful tool in your toolkit. It is the scalpel of complexity reduction. It is something you want to be consistently thinking about as you work your way through the process of redefining your business.

Quad 1 forms the economic core of the business. Is it being managed as such? As the general manager of the business you need to identify and review whether to eliminate products and customers that interfere with the core of the business contained in Quad 1. There will be plenty to eliminate; however, this is never an easy task. Turning down an order or eliminating a product is difficult especially when you have spent your entire career fighting to get every single order/customer. Upper management may have a vested interest in a product or customer so it can also become political. If you are methodical and objective, however, you can trim your product offering without significantly altering your overall gross margin. This is where the data helps drive the decision making process.

Major operational streamlining breakthroughs typically occur only after going through the line simplification process.

Going back to our refrigerator model—if you have two ketchups—do you really need both? If you have a 12 oz. bottle and a jumbo 50 oz. bottle—why do you have both? Do you need ketchup that is red and green, especially when you are spending a tremendous amount of time sorting through the refrigerator trying to find the bread and meat because you have so many ketchup bottles? As silly as this may sound, this is exactly what happens in many companies; it is simply labeled differently.

Quad 2, for example, is replete with opportunities to consolidate SKUs into Quad 1 Product Offerings, but you need the support and focus of sales. The sales force needs to embrace the line simplification process and contribute their understanding of what the market requires. The key is a solid understanding of the core attributes your product is delivering to your customer. Product variations exist for a reason, but you must divide these attributes into essential and non-essential. Static-free may be critical, but color options, a double pack, or an extra ¼″ size variation may not.

Why would the organization be interested in selling fewer items? Because you are going to get much better at providing/manufacturing the products you do sell. These items will be in stock and available at a much lower cost structure. If you need to be competitive on an item you will have the cost infrastructure to outperform your competition. Finally, once you have trimmed up the entire excess product offering, you will have a chance to go back and carefully decide where you will invest your time and money. You **will** have more time and money after this process.

Within Quad 3 the primary focus is on marketing and distribution channels. You are looking at customers and markets that have higher transaction costs relative to the revenue they bring earn when compared to your Quad 1. The goal is to find customers who are in Quad 3 but can move up to Quad 1 through the sale of additional products. You can want to go through their product purchases and see what other Quad 1 items you can sell to them. On the other hand, you might consolidate some Quad 3 customers by requesting that they purchase from a Quad 1 customers. This will simplify your business while improving your relationship with your Quad 1 customer. You want to avoid having Quad 3 customers interfere with your ability to manage your Quad 1. An example of this would be a Quad 3 customer that purchases all of your inventory of a specific item every three months and then you need to back order that item for your Quad 1 customers. Developing a system or incentive that encouraged Quad 3 customers to smooth their ordering activity would have an additional benefit of improving service to your Quad 1 customers.

Quad 4 usually proves the richest in terms of insight and elimination opportunities. These tend to be your highest transaction cost items for your company. Sometimes, companies will interrupt a continuous production run of a core product to manufacture a non-core product for a non-core customer because a customer is particularly vocal. Too often top management is the guilty party in this situation.

80/20 analyses and Quad mapping are a foundation for judicious management decisions, not a license to sidestep thinking. It is naïve to presume that the answer to the non-core products and non-core customers constituting Quad 4 is their wholesale elimination. Some of these non-core products may be the future of the business. The same can be said of non-core customers. What you don't want to do is just simply look to eliminate Quad 4. You need to understand why the customers and products exist and how you can best simplify them. This may mean elimination, but only after careful scrutiny.

It is usually in this step of the process that the transformation runs into its biggest resistance. Only a few people will have the ability to see an end game and where it might lead. We've learned that:

The simplification of a business is complex.

The line simplification process is time consuming, because it has to be methodical. Skeptics will challenge the process and claim that it can't demonstrate or illustrate the hypothetical payoffs.

Expect to hear seemingly reasonable objections such as:

- "How can this small item have any impact on the business overall?"

- "This product only takes 20 minutes to manufacture; how can it affect anyone?"

- "Why are we wasting time on any of this? Let's get back to the important customers/products?"

- "But we make 70% margin on the product.

- "My customers are going to be really upset."

The answer is that this is all noise and until you strip away the noise you can't effectively judge the orchestra. The first stage of this process is a gedanken experiment; all of the choices are hypothetical and reversible. Exhibit 18 suggests one way to view line simplification as an iterative discovery and design process.

Exhibit 18
Managing Line Simplification as an Iterative Process

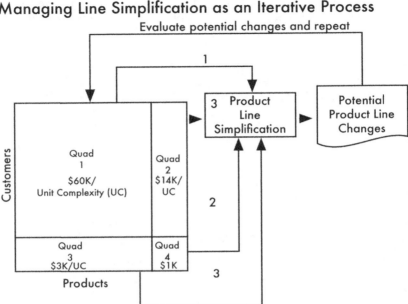

Be aggressive about clearing the outliers and eliminating product. It is only after you have cleared away the noise that game-changing opportunities will come into sight. This calls for patience. Those outside the process, especially the skeptics, find it hard to see where the process is going while the loss of revenue is readily apparent. Even within the process, it is important to keep an open mind. First, it is a search for simplicity at little or no cost. Later, it can create the space and resources for more aggressive, even radical, change.

When management objects to the loss of customers you need to remind people that these are going to be primarily Quad 4 customers that aren't contributing much gross margin. Through it all, you are searching for opportunities. If we could rebuild the business from scratch to best fit a business that dealt exclusively with Quad 1 customers and products, what would the new business look like?

How Deep To Cut—Fat, Muscle Or Bone?

The objective is to eliminate as many SKU's as possible without impacting the needs of your Quad 1 customers while simultaneously having minimal impact on total gross margin. What is minimal? This tends to be around 2-4% of total gross margin. More dramatic line simplification cuts can run as high as 5%-6%. Moving beyond 5-6% of total gross margin requires a deep understanding of the impact on customers and infrastructure.

The simplification brought to the business through this process will yield far great returns. The primary purpose is not about hitting a gross margin reduction target. It is about simplifying product offerings without impacting Quad 1 customers. These numbers are generally what we have seen occur in practice.

Reducing the number of SKU's by 30% to 40% is another worthy target. Shifting a customer from one product offering to another, for example, can reduce SKUs as one form of line simplification while preserving and possibly reducing the impact on gross margin.

Line simplification opportunities surface in multiple ways:

- Similar products different packaging (especially private label).
- Similar products different packaging quantities.
- Different products serving the same market applications.
- Different colors requiring separate SKU's and inventory.
- Unnecessary parts offering.
- Products that haven't sold in several years.
- Parts for products that haven't sold in years.
- Low selling products that are difficult to manufacture.
- Low selling products with difficult customers who don't pay their invoices on time.
- R&D projects that never sold but no one is willing to call it because it was top management's pet project.
- Low selling products that don't fit your core competencies.
- Low selling products that are very complex to manufacture and/or distribute which don't suite your core competencies.

You also look for the following Customer opportunities for line simplification:

- Customers that don't fit your 80/20 distribution channel that require special products.
- Customers that are outside of your geographical range.
- Customers with exceptionally low margin.

- Customers that have high transaction costs (small frequent orders).

This is all about making your business simpler to manage. Often from a marketing standpoint it is about taking a smaller customer and having them purchase through an existing Quad 1 customer. You may lose a little margin, but you have simplified your business.

An enormous amount of complexity seeps into companies. The complexity is often so interwoven that it becomes virtually invisible; it becomes a part of the fabric of the organization. More importantly it distracts you from focusing on your Quad 1. Once you have gone through the line simplification process and examined what remains in your business, then you can see the true drivers of your company.

Once implemented, it allows you to start to restructure the business, particularly the manufacturing, service aspects of your company, around the remaining Quad 1 core drivers. Returning to our refrigerator analogy, you want your bread and meat front and center so that you never run out. In other words, you cannot survive on ketchup, so you don't want to place it in the front shelf, and you definitely don't want five varieties obscuring your view (well maybe Heinz does).

Trend Tracker in a March 2003 article, "The War on Complexity," offers this perspective:

> *"by proliferating products, customers, suppliers, services, locations, etc. All of these defocus management efforts, waste valuable time and money, and reduce shareholder value. Even through the problem is destroying corporate profitability, it has evaded everyone's radar screens because none of the current corporate metrics account for complexity".[11]*

Product Line Simplification in Action

Several years back we applied line simplification to a division of a company with over 8,000 SKU's. As we looked at the stack of papers listing all of the products, the enormity of the task weighed on the room. The consensus was that they had already tried this several times before and had always run into stiff resistance from the sales team. This time we had a mandate from a new CEO to work our way through the product offerings since the business unit was only performing in the low single digits for operating income and they were constantly struggling to get product out the door.

After sorting through products with an 80/20 analysis, we reduced SKU's to 2000 items with only a 2% reduction in total Gross Margin. Obviously, there were an enormous number of non-performing SKU's. Even this 2% reduction was suspect because it was believed that the customers would migrate to a comparable remaining product.

During these meetings there was much vocal support for the number of existing SKU's, criticism that we didn't understand the market and predictions that customers would give a lot of push back. Being attentive to the concerns of the management team, we developed a list of proposed product eliminations and shared the list with selected Quad 1 customers. This was done both as a reality check of the market and as a way to develop acceptance from the existing sales management team that had resisted any SKU eliminations over the years.

Feedback from customers surprised everyone. These customers had been waiting for a product line reduction and embraced the recommendations. Their view was that the product offering was too complex and left them uncertain about what to purchase. Only the sales representatives, not the customers, were concerned with reducing products.

Empowered by this additional input we dug deeper to discover that the bulk of the 2,000 SKUs were a private labeling issue for several Quad 1 customers and in essence there were only 500 unique products from a manufacturing point of view.

Reducing the product catalog from 8,000 to 500 SKUs allowed managers and staff to believe that they might actually manage the business in a different way. While another 80/20 analysis revealed that 100 SKUs within the 500 accounted for 80% of total margin, the group nonetheless concluded that eliminating 7,500 SKUs was a sufficient starting point for the first round.

This simplification process enabled the company to set-up a totally different, visual, pull through production system. This system wouldn't have worked with 8000 SKU's; there simply wasn't enough wall space. After the first year, the company had improved net income to 15%, moving them from being a poor performer to one of the best. The on-time delivery issue also disappeared so the Quad 1 customers were pleased with the results.

The lesson here is the power of anchoring line simplification in the data. Anchoring the process in the data counters the myths and legacy issues that exist at most organizations. When in doubt, talk to your Quad 1 customers.

Managing Through the Transition

Identifying and isolating items in line simplification is important, but managing the execution and transition with the broader organization and your customers is essential. The goal is to persuade customers that they have as much to gain from simplification as you do. For the rest of the organization, that has yet to be significantly engaged in the effort, the project team faces a parallel problem of persuading the organization that there is a better business on the other side.

Starting the product review process in Quad 1 is not only logically correct, it is also organizationally and emotionally correct. It allows you to focus on what you will build on for the future. Consensus around Quad 1 tends to build quickly. This is helpful for the cross functional team looking at it. As you work through Quad 1 you will find issues that impose constraints as well as define your core competencies. It's generally easier to understand the significance of the analyses and to agree on priorities. Value Streams are successfully carved out. There is generally consensus and little to no objection to starting with the core of the business.

After Quad 1, we have found that it often makes the most sense to turn to Quad 4. It is the realm of customers and products past their prime or those that never found themselves. But it can also be the source of future gems. For the most part, you will find that Quad 4 fails to add value commensurate with the management problems/complexity it generates. You absolutely must go through this Quad Systematically – SKU by SKU, Customer by Customer.

Within Quad 4, it tends to be easier to drive toward consensus on which actions make straightforward sense and which may require additional analysis. Working in Quad 4 also helps the team and the organization develop its analytical muscle and its collective decision making prowess.

This is good when we then turn our attention to Quads 2 and 3. These are where many of the most difficult conversations and decisions lie. Customers and Products in these Quads have supporters and potential. However, there are often both analytical and political issues to be worked through. Tackling the remaining challenges in Quads 2 and 3 is easier now that we have the experience from Quads 1 and 4 to draw on and now that we have freed up resources from those efforts that can be redirected to the opportunities of moving the customers and products in Quads 2 and 3 towards a future in Quad 1.

It is during this process that the project team must begin interacting with the rest of the organization routinely. The potential simplification steps identified during this process need to be sanity checked with managers across the organization. Exhibit 19 depicts the interaction that begins to evolve between the project team and the organization as a whole.

Exhibit 19
Testing Line Simplification Opportunities with the Existing Operation

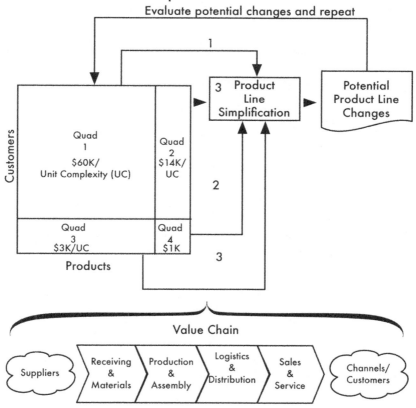

You will need to change your organization to capitalize on the opportunities identified during the line simplification process. More critically, you must also change the way you do business with many of your customers. Approaches that work include

- Identify substitute products in your Quad 1 or Quad 2 and recommend them to your customers. Provide scripts to both sales and customer service to smooth the transition. Don't simply announce that you have eliminated a product.

- Consolidate two Quad 2 products to create a new product that falls into Quad 1. In this case, it is about convincing customers to move from one product SKU to another. You need a simple, compelling story. Selected large customers will need to be contacted individually.

- Raise prices substantially on marginal products and let the market decide if this is something you should be selling.

- Tell customers that you are no longer selling those products. Refer them to a supplier that doesn't carry products that compete with your Quad 1.

- Manufacture a safety stock and tell customers that you no longer make the product. Allow customers that complain to draw from the safety stock reducing the impact and giving them time to deal with it.

- If you are on the edge, continue to manufacture the product for your larger customers and consider it a cost of servicing these customers.

Line simplification is about finding a better balance with your products and your customers. There is no cookie cutter approach. Each situation takes a thorough review. It is also an iterative process as you work through a business. There is no requirement to execute all the simplification at once. You can apply line simplification cautiously at first and more aggressively as the team becomes comfortable with the process.

CHAPTER 7
SOLVING FOR PATTERN—REDESIGNING YOUR COMPANY

We always find complexity without a corresponding economic payoff in our clients. Quad analysis and the line simplification process reveal the elements of the business that form its core. The Quad analysis clusters products and customers based on their economic performance. Line simplification clears away the underbrush. There is a strategic opportunity now to redesign around that core before moving on to the specific tactical improvements using the tools in the following chapter. We think of this effort as "solving for pattern."

Resist the temptation, often advocated in lean initiatives, to simply drive forward, focus on obvious problems, ride employees harder, cut expenses, and ratchet up quotas. This can generate short-term profits and temporary improvement but the end result will be regression to the mean. Organizational systems, by design or by evolution, are balanced to operate best at a certain rhythm or cadence. You must re-balance the system to make a sustainable transformation in the throughput or output of an organization. You need to transform the system to re-balance the system.

At this point, the team has hovered over and slogged through the data, classified products and customers by quadrant, walked the plant floor or service counters observing how products and customers are produced and served, and generated an inventory of line simplification opportunities. This next step is about perceiving and identifying patterns that exist in products and markets. Discovering and exploiting these patterns yields big impact on the bottom line.

Think about your business without preconception. Start with Quad 1. Take a step back from the intensity of the project and the myriad of details to discern broader patterns. Sit in the team room with the Quad data posted and exposed around the walls. Walk through the plant floor and operations areas again. Sense the flow and pulse of the organization. Look for that game changing, out of the box transformation.

We always find something impactful. It is hidden in the data and discovered as you integrate the diverse experiences of the team and knowledge of the organization and operations. Your floor walks will confirm it. For your particular business, we can't tell you exactly what it is; just that the opportunities are there.

Working through the line simplification process and focusing the business around the core products and customers who constitute Quad 1 will provide you with better insight into your business. With many products and customers eliminated and your core focus well-defined, you want to look for alternative structures for managing your business. Getting ready to launch change is a time of intense focus. The project team better grasps how the pieces of the organization could fit together. Now is the time to pause and reflect on these lessons and look for radical alternatives. This is opportunity to develop and implement game changing transformations.

Also identify the complexities that have developed to keep the system in balance. Which are essential and which are accidental? Accidental complexities develop to fix problems or anomalies. Someone in shipping who double checks every shipping label because one shipment to a vocal customer went astray two years ago is an example of an accidental complexity. Accidental complexities are symptoms of a deeper problem. Find and address the underlying problem, not the symptom. Essential complexity can be a strength rather than a problem. You just need to identify it and develop systems to better manage it.

Finding Levers—Building an Economic Model

In the course of carrying out the 80/20 and Quad analyses, the team has recast data from multiple systems of record into a series of spreadsheets that capture the basic economics of the organization in terms of products and customers. During the line simplification process and as you apply the tools and techniques in the next chapter, you need to review and assess the impact of different options on performance.

The spreadsheets you have developed to this point can be extended into a simple economic operating model of the business that supports this review and assessment. Additional data can be added to the spreadsheets to develop a more comprehensive view of the organization. While it can take a little time to set-up, the additional data exists somewhere in the organization. Key items that might be included in a model:

- Revenue.

- Contribution Margin.

- Quantity Sold.

- Quad Assignments.

- Processes used in the manufacturing of the products.

- Equipment used.

- Throughput and setup time on required equipment.

- Manufactured or purchased.

- Formulations or Raw Material Requirements.

- Warehouse Space Requirements.

- Equipment/Technical Needs to Make the Product.

- Method of Delivery of the products—Different Distribution Channels.

- Safety/Regulatory Issues.

- Geographical Manufacturing Issues.

- Geographical Selling Issues.

- End-User Markets/Industries.

- Customers purchasing product.

Organize the model by Product SKU. The model then becomes your discussion platform as you evaluate options to redeploy your manufacturing/service platform assets. Use the model to identify and isolate barriers to possible reorganizations of the operation. Look for unrecognized patterns that exist in your business. Are there similarities in process steps, machinery use, or material flow that might be exploited? Are there old constraints or limits that no longer exist?

Swimming around in the data and searching for patterns is critical. When you find an inclusive pattern where a lot of the products, equipment, and customers have the same relationship then you flip to the other side and look at what is not included in this mix.

Quad 1 Opportunities

This is the time to think inside each box beginning with Quad 1. What would you do differently if Quad 1 were the entire business? Can you aggregate or separate your products so that they can have dedicated equipment and processes? Are there certain customers that are purchasing the same grouping of products? Do your top products all use the same raw material input? As you identify patterns, don't contaminate Quad 1 with Quad 4 just because they have similar processes. During this process people have a tendency to revert to their existing framework within an organization.

This process can be exceptionally powerful as you discover patterns. The model is a great brain storming tool as you sort and review your data and find things in patterns and then find the SKU's that are out of pattern and why. These patterns allow you to go back to your toolkit and augment your product line simplification process. You are trying to find value streams that run through your company from start to finish. These value streams are critical to the process and once you find them then you can build your business around the SKU's that make up these value streams. Value stream would be a group of products that have similar raw material, equipment, technical skills, or packaging requirements.

One example of this was in a plastics business where we were looking at the allocation of extruder capacity, resin types, freight expense, geographical location, and warehouse space to determine if it was possible to take an existing business that was managed according to extruder capacity and see if it could be broken into several different business units each with their own facility, management structure, etc.

To build the model, we integrated the Quad Analysis with warehouse data, manufacturing data and safety data. Through this process we were able to determine the allocation of extruders and set-ups. Using the model we were able to simulate a structure that dedicated equipment to a single Quad 1 product and allowed the operation to use Kanban and Visual Management techniques that had once been rejected as infeasible. The model not only determined the structure of the final system, but it first served to establish that the approach was feasible and highly attractive economically.

Quad 2 Opportunities

Quad 2 items are products that you need to support your primary customers. You want to look at the assets that are used to make the Quad 2 products and try to carve these out separately. You don't want to interrupt a major job to manufacture a minor product.

It isn't just the cost of the set-up and interruption that drives the cost, but it is the fact that you can't develop systems around your Quad 1 products. During one conversion job of a company – this took a lot of explanation, but it wasn't until we allocated a section of the manufacturing assets to a product group where we were able to develop a system around it.

Even though the line was running only 80% of the time because we had stripped out the other 20% of the work and placed on another dedicated piece of equipment—we were able to downstream the converting and packaging section of the business. In the end we produced the same amount of product just a lot faster.

Once this system was in place—new and innovative processes were created. Sometimes folks just need to see the process in place to come up with the best ideas. In many situations you will get your best ideas from the exact people who were resistant to the change in the first place.

Quad 2 items need to be provided to your customer. You want to set-up manufacturing systems that allow for quick change over, bring a lot of flexibility to the down-stream activities and are often less efficient in the manufacturing process. Quad 2 products can also be items that you can't manufacture in a continuous nature you might need to build stock with some type of production trigger. Usually a simple min/max system will work since you want to balance the inventory carrying costs against the set-up and run time. Typically the set-up and run time are more expensive portions of this equation.

You may find that a lot of these jobs can be outsourced to other companies. You want to review what you are doing in Quad 1 (what you are good at) and try not to do something different in the Quad 2. However, what you absolutely don't want to do is put another company in the business with the potential of serving your Quad 1 Customers. If you need to do something different in Quad 2—then you want to isolate these processes and don't let them contaminate the Quad 1.

Quad 3 Opportunities

This section is more about looking at existing operations of your core driver customers and products. Quad 3 customers, by definition, are purchasing existing products that you have the systems and structures in place to deliver easily. As you go through this process and redesign your value streams and look for major opportunities, you want to make certain that you are meeting the needs the of Quad 3 without interfering with your Quad 1. If you are using visual triggers to manufacture product, then you want to build in the ability to service your Quad 3 customers. You just need to keep their needs in mind when you are building your systems.

One example of this was a manufacturing company that had a large parts business for existing equipment that was being manufactured on the line. The parts businesses tended to be mostly Quad 3 service companies, but when they came in and purchased parts they would do so in large volume.

As the company went over to a full Kanban, visual system it was critical that the Quad 3 parts business was built into the Quad 1 systems. Otherwise, they were either shutting down the production line because of part shortages or they were impacting the ability of these third party repair shops to service Quad 1 customers' equipment.

Quad 4 Opportunities

Here you just need a solid understanding of the outliers and how you manage them. If they made it past the line simplification process, then you have found merit in retaining them. You want to isolate these and look for opportunities to simplify or outsource. In some cases, you might carve this outside of your core business both physically and structurally.

These also offer an opportunity to outsource. The key is to isolate them so they don't interfere with your Quad 1 customers. If these represent future growth products that haven't had time to mature then you might dedicate a team to develop them rather than having them managed through you existing management; especially if they are items that don't fit into current market channels.

This is the place where you would apply your crossover threshold rate to the various projects to see if you should continue to explore them. If in the end these products or customers don't have the potential to reach Quad 1, then you should eliminate them.

Using the Model to Explore Scenarios

As you explore the quads, this is your chance to build different scenarios and value streams that are out of the box. The benefit to the model is that it allows you to address the potential issues of manufacturing or servicing before making actual changes to the operation.

The other key take away is that this is an iterative process. There is no one right answer. The model allows you to explore different "right answers". Often the actions taken will depend upon other actions. You might decide to eliminate a Quad 4 product because it would interfere with the Quad 1 production layout in one scenario but you might keep it under another scenario because it wouldn't interfere.

PART 3
USING THE TOOLKIT
EFFECTIVELY

CHAPTER 8
THE TOOLKIT

As you work through the various opportunities that surface during the Quad Analysis, Product Line Simplification and Economic Modeling, there are an assortment of relevant tools and techniques that are a your disposal at different points and Quads. In this chapter we have organized, assembled, and described the tools that we typically draw upon to transform a company. Some of them are new while many are tried and true except that we tend to follow a slightly different path.

Basic Lean Tools such as SQDC boards, 5S, Shadow Boards and Single Minute Exchange of Dies (SMED), and Six Sigma are mentioned in passing during different parts of our discussion. However, the primary focus of most of these lean techniques is to treat the symptoms of complexity rather than the cause. While many of these lean techniques are helpful, they have been discussed at length in other venues so we will only discuss them here as required. Our focus is on tools that help root out the cause of the complexity rather than trying to manage it. In properly performing your product line simplification you have taken a necessary step in helping to successfully streamline your business.

In the table that follows we have grouped tools into a handful of broader categories to simplify finding and applying tools as you work. Following that, for each tool, there is a standardized definition and description of each tool, the quadrants where it is most applicable, and the likely benefits. We also provide examples of the use of the tools, the questions you should ask, and checklists of considerations when you implement them.

Many of the tools are symbiotic. When you use three or four of them together it is transformative in an exponential way. Phenomenally more transformative than if you just use one or two alone in an isolated approach.

Exhibit 20
The Toolkit

Operational/Servicing Policies: Redesigning Your Company around Your Quads

- In-Lining Operations
- Dedicated Equipment
- One At A Time Manufacturing
- Decentralized Leads: Autonomy, Ownership and Empowerment
- Daily Value Stream Walks (Gemba Walks)

Inventory Control and Management Techniques

- Kanban Inventory Management Systems
- Raw Material Kanban
- C-Class Inventory: (Applying 80/20 Thinking To Inventory)
- Consolidation Of Raw Material

Vendor Collaboration

- Vendor Education
- Vendor Consolidation
- Rolling Purchase Order System (RPOS)
- Overseas Vendors
- Market Rate Of Demand (Pull through System)

Company Wide Simplification

- Outsourcing
- Sales, Marketing And Price
- Transactional Analysis (Stapling Yourself To An Order)
- Point Of Use
- Triad Business Structure
- Cross Over Thresholds

Visual Systems

Throughout the discussion of specific tools, you will see frequent references to making workflows and information throughout operations visual. One of the most powerful weapons against complexity is visibility. It is the underlying premise behind adages such as "a place for everything and everything in its place."

The human visual system is adept at recognizing patterns and noticing anomalies; effective operations and control systems exploit that capability. The Kanban two-bin system for managing parts inventories—which we discuss shortly—is an easily understood example. Divide the supply of some part, such as machine screws, into two side-by-side bins. As soon as one bin is empty, order more machine screws. Anyone can see whether a bin is empty or not empty; no one needs to count items to make a decision.

Regardless of the individual tool or technique, look for opportunities to take advantage of our innate skill at seeing what surrounds us. Design work flows so that problems or interruptions create a visible break in the action. Wherever possible, make it easy for anyone and everyone to see what is going on within a plant or facility. Get key data and metrics out of tiny computer screens and up on a wall or whiteboard in front of the people who need and use it the most.

The more evident and obvious you can make the visual cues, the more you empower to react and fix a problem when it occurs.

CHAPTER 9
OPERATIONAL/SERVICING POLICIES

In-Lining Operations

DESCRIPTION

In-lining is the process of setting up your physical operations so that work and/or service flows in the simplest, most sequential path possible.

The flow of material and work through your operations should be optimized. This is not a difficult concept, nor one that is particularly new. The difference here is that you want to start by focusing exclusively on your core products and core customers that make up Quad 1. Often this clearest path is obscured by non-Quad 1 products and customers. Don't allow other Quads to interfere with making the right choice for your Quad 1.

Start with the primary components for your operations whether it be people, steel, stampings, coffee, aluminum, tubing, resin or any other service. Lay out the manufacturing process sequentially on the floor with tools and equipment arranged as you would use them. As you go, figure out the tools and equipment needed to keep things moving through the cell or facility. What you will find is that smaller, dedicated equipment (we will discuss later) is often better than large multi-purpose equipment that can perform every task.

Often legacy decisions will have created a sub-optimal layout especially in situations where the equipment and service have been added incrementally over time. Many organizations have their equipment arranged by function rather than by value stream. This was done originally under the mistaken belief that the efficient use of equipment, skills and infra-structure where so needed to support a specific production operation that it was better to keep everything in one area.

Think about it like your house – you don't have all of your beds in one room, dressers in another room and televisions in a third room. You have them distributed so that each family member can use them in the most efficient manner. Why then would you have all of your drill presses, laminators, and sorters in the same area?

The stock answer is that they have similar infrastructure needs like power, exhaust, and/or operator skill. But you wouldn't make the argument that all of the showers in a house be placed in the same room due to plumbing complexity. You might place the bathrooms back to back – but you certainly would have them separated and available to multiple users.

In setting up this type of process you are creating the infrastructure for a pull through inventory system; a concept we will discuss later in more detail.

Also in the process of setting up your lines – you want to bring as much balance to work flow as possible so that each step/process requires just about the same amount of time as the next step and/process. The ideal situation is one where the part/product/service person flows through the line as you perform each additional task or service. When this can't happen then you create some type of buffer system to insulate the sections from one another. You want to remove bottlenecks where one particular part of the process restricts the flow through other processes.

APPLICABLE QUADS

This tool is most powerful with Quad 1. When production is totally in-lined and moves seamlessly, sequentially through the plant you are at your optimum. You want to arrange your facilities so that you can consistently deliver your core product in the most efficient manner. It is acceptable if some machinery sits idle for a day because the overall through put of the organization will increase dramatically when you properly in-line. It isn't about producing more stuff; it is about meeting the needs of your customers.

The manufacturing or servicing requirements of Quad 2 and Quad 4 may be such that you can't in-line their processes, but this is acceptable. These Quads may need a different skill set than your Quad 1 and it doesn't yield the same kind of improvement in gross margin as your Quad 1 does for the investment in time and money.

You will want to in-line some of your Quad 2 and 4 production, but the focus needs to be on producing these in such a way that they don't interfere with your Quad 1.

RELATED TOOLS

The in-lining process works even more powerfully when it is combined with the dedicated equipment and a strong Kanban inventory management system where product is created in a pull through system

Kanban—Inventory Management Systems

Produce at Pull-through Production Rate

Dedicated Equipment

BENEFITS

In-lining processes makes it easy to see and time where people are using their time. By breaking work down sequentially and watching the flow it is then simple to perform a time study on what parts of the process are most time consuming and complex. Inefficient operations and investment opportunities are readily apparent. Employees will think you are doing them a huge service because you are making their jobs easier.

In-lining also eliminates the waste of walking to procure inventory or waiting for a material handler to bring the inventory to you.

One of the secondary benefits of in-lining is handling a surge of orders in a particular value stream. You can shift people to the line and have them work in parallel with each other to get the maximum output (the slowest part of the line limits the rate of work flow through the entire line). If properly balanced, everyone is working at a consistent pace happily churning out product. An in-lined process is inherently more amenable to being ramped up and ramped down. The reason for this is that you immediately start to trigger production on the line as parts are passed from one area to the next. With a functional approach things are moved around the company in batches and tend to dominate an area for a while.

EXAMPLES

In one company, we had a process of taking steel castings, machining them and then sending them out for secondary processes (heat treatment and black oxide). When the parts came back, we would then perform the assembly process. This was a multi-step process requiring a lot of transactions, inventory, and redundant handling. The decision was made to inline. We found that the secondary processes were causing the most complexity. After challenging some of the basic beliefs in the company, it was found that if we made certain investments and modified the secondary processes then we could bring the parts in already heat treated and black oxided. Several people in the organization felt that it wasn't possible to machine parts in this state. However, with a little persistence and creativity it worked.

This was a huge simplification success because the products previously flowed through machining in large batches requiring an enormous amount of planning. With the in-lining process in place, we manufactured product as we needed it. We also eliminated a tremendous number of transactions that used to occur each day on our products. First, we had to realize what was our core business, look at how we would set up the in-lined process and then figure out what were our obstacles to solving them. In the end, we were able to successfully inline the entire process. This in-lining process allowed us to improve efficiency by over 30%.

Another example of successful in-lining is the flow that has been developed within Starbucks. First you take the order and pay for the product, next you move down a station where someone provides you with your cup of coffee, then you are moved over to another area to mix your flavorings (so the final process has been set-up in such a way as to have the customer perform it). And what happens when you run out of Half and Half? The customer actually walks the container over to the counter and exchanges it for a new one that is already set-up and ready to go. You are moved through the process step by step, not allowing any one place to have too much accumulation of tasks.

QUESTIONS

- Is your facility set-up by function or by value stream?

- Would you set-up your facility differently if you were to focus on just your Quad 1 products?

- Do you have redundant material movement throughout your facility (especially raw material or packaging)?

- Do the same people who run the equipment have control over the access to the raw material and packaging?

- Are there people dedicated to the planning process who reside outside of the plant floor (planners)?

- Do you have people dedicated to strictly moving things around the plant (material handlers)?

- When you walk your facility – does it have a natural, sequential flow to it?

- Is this natural flow set-up around your Quad 1 products and customers?

- Could an outside person understand the entire process in a five-minute walk?

- How often do your Quad 2 and 4 interfere with the Quad 1 process?

- How often is your core raw material handled before being used in the production process?

CHECKLIST

- Develop strong understanding of the flow of your Quad 1 products.

- Look at the steps, processes, and equipment involved in each process. Identify the needs of the process and identify where shared resources are creating unwarranted interference.

- Compare these steps and process to your existing layout.

- Determine what fits in a sequential flow and what doesn't and why.

- If the consensus is that something can't be in-lined, figure out why and then break it down to the root cause and work your way through it so it can be.

- Look for additional SKU's and/or customers where the process involved in the delivery of the service or the manufacturing of the product are similar.

- Develop a high level layout of the ideal in-lined processes.

Dedicated Equipment

DESCRIPTION

Dedicated Equipment is simply assigning equipment, set-ups and/or people to perform similar jobs over and over again avoiding the expense and complexity that comes with change over and interference. You want to undertake this process with the primary focus being on dedicating equipment to your Quad 1.

Dedicated Equipment can be an extremely powerful tool for simplification. You can properly organize the systems and flow around your core products. It isn't until you strip away a lot of the noise that the apparent benefit reveals itself. Smaller, less expensive equipment is often a better solution. Rather than purchasing one machine that can do everything, you should purchase several smaller, simpler machines that can be dedicated.

APPLICABLE QUADS

This tool also works best for your Quad 1 products. The key is having a strong understanding of the process, products, and customer demands. As you dedicate equipment you want to remove the Quad 2 and 4 products from the process so that you can eliminate set-up, QC checks or other variables that enter the equation due to change over. For your Quad 2 and Quad 4 products you are going to be looking for more flexibility on the equipment so you can easily change in and out of runs.

Start strictly with the Quad 1 items and try to isolate value streams that can be in-lined with dedicated equipment. It is ok if you aren't always using the equipment or you have sections of the company that are shut down from time to time. Again your objective is to match your customer's order requirements not run at 100% capacity.

RELATED TOOLS

Dedicated Equipment works best when the lines have been properly in-lined and have a strong visual Kanban system. The Point of Use tool is also critical here because once you have dedicated equipment to a process you want to make certain it is a part of the flow of the value stream. You want to make certain the inventory or service is close by so it is visual and readily accessible to the operators.

SMED (Single Minute Exchange of a Die) is one lean tool has that had been deployed to mitigate the time lost in change-over. This is usually completed as a Kaizen event where you break down the process of changing out a die into internal and external components. Internal being those items that have to be done when the machine is not running and external being those items that you can do when the machine is running. You focus on the external items and figure out how to get these items completed a head of time. This is a straightforward process with the key example always being pit crews in car racing.

SMED can be very successful and help to break down batch processes, but it doesn't address the fact that you still have changeover. The fastest change over is no change over at all. You can often achieve this with the proper line simplification and dedicated equipment. Obviously you need to have some common sense to the entire process. If you can't set-up dedicated equipment then you are still going to have to make items in a batch process. Understanding your process flow and pushing to get the work to dedicated equipment with one-piece flow is key. The fastest set-up is no set-up at all.

SMED also applies across the entire company. You want to look at the data and find variables that impact you across the entire production cycle and figure out ways to shorten these or set-up systems that allow you to migrate from one process to another in the most seamless manner.

This is exceptionally critical as you try to drive down your finished goods inventory to improve your return on invested capital. There is a direct correlation between the cost of a product changeover and the amount of inventory you need to carry on your floor in finished goods. The shorter/less expensive the change over, the more you can decrease your production runs so you can be more reactive to your customer's needs. By being effective here—you can have a major impact on your inventory dollars.

Unfortunately, there are certain processes in chemical, plastics, and paper manufacturing where instantaneous change over is impossible to achieve because the equipment and process in and of itself requires a batch process to run. For example, in manufacturing plastic resin you may need a certain volume of product to create the proper chemical reactions to manufacture the product. However, such processes are rare. With most of these processes you can at least perform the final packaging one at a time.

In-Lining Operations

Point Of Use

Kanban—Inventory Management Systems

BENEFITS

Dedicated Equipment is one of your most powerful tools to improve the efficiency of your business. Within each section of your plant, look at the needs of each worker and determine what they need to get their job done. If there are related tools needed to operate the equipment then these should remain at the workstation preferably with some type of 5S Shadow Board. (Shadow Board is a technique to keep the tools and equipment required at a workstation visual and accessible). The intention is not to be setting up the machine on a regular basis. You want the machine dedicated to performing one task.

With dedicated equipment you look at the motion and movement within each cell and figure out what is the best way to perform each function. Whether this be pouring a cup of coffee or adding pneumatic equipment, you are always looking for motion and figuring out how to streamline it (tool balancers, sliders, etc.).

You also want to analyze the way you manufacture your product and figure out how to strip work out of the process by changing the final design. This can have a major impact on the cost of making the product. A strong engineer with operational experience can have a major impact.

It doesn't matter whether the task takes up a lot of time—if it is repetitive, then you want to eliminate it. Often the equipment doesn't have to be very expensive.

Also you want to get the tools and equipment in place so that your workers stay in their general area. Ideally, you would like to have your employees stay on their line and remain in their area for the entire day, manufacturing product.

Dedicated equipment is exceptionally productive since:

- Your production time is nearly 100% value-added.

- You eliminate an enormous amount of quality control checking. You don't have first article inspection anymore because your equipment doesn't change.

- You can take your consumable items that you use with the equipment and place it next to the equipment and set-up in a Kanban system (Kanbans).

There may be opportunities to dedicate groups or classes. Maybe you could run the same resin on the same extruder or the same size sheet to avoid the most expensive changeovers.

Since you are manufacturing product and immediately using it in your production or assembly process since you are in-lined with dedicated equipment, mistakes or errors are caught almost immediately. You typically have a shorter QC process at the end of the line with this type of system. So you are constantly checking the product to guarantee they are meeting your QC standards.

Hopefully you have dedicated equipment again for the QC tasks. You also achieve a consistent product flow so that you are able to eliminate inventory in your company. You don't have inventory queued up in front of equipment for a change over. Finally, you have your production line and you are able to cross train people all the way up and down the line you can make the work more interesting. The cross training is easier because using dedicated equipment you are able to strip out a lot of the more complex components in a process.

Employees that work a line typically seem happier; they have some diversity in their work. They can see their daily production. They are in control. They can improve the process and enjoy the benefits. Everyone wins.

EXAMPLES

Working with a large extruding company trying to figure out how best to streamline their product lines provides one example of the value of dedicated equipment. They had multiple extrusion lines with various jobs being moved in and out of the lines. The work was organized to maximize throughput of the extruders. Everyone seemed exceptionally busy and there was a full time person dedicated to gathering up the production books every single day for the pending jobs. Another team focused on production planning.

This created a lot of product turnover for the machines, but kept them running 24/7. On the downstream side of the extruding process the company had become very good at moving various packaging products and rewinders in and out across varying lines. It was impressive to watch.

Based on a Quad Analysis we determined that we could dedicate one extruder to their largest running product. The packaging materials used for these SKUs were then taken and arranged at the end of the line. By dedicating this line, we could store the packaging items along the line making inventory management much more visual and eliminating the need to use a material handler to move things in and out of the line. It turned out that this particular line would only be required to run 80% of the time when dedicated to this one product. It took management a while to accept the fact that the line might actually be shut down during the week. What they had missed was that they were already shut down during the week due to all of the changeovers.

We then took the other product that was being run on the first extruder, moved it to another extruder, and in-lined the rewinding equipment. Again, this particular extruder ended up running 75% rather than 100% of the time. However, they actually saw more through-put when they had the dedicated equipment. We were able to eliminate most of the changeovers and get more efficient production out of each line. Not only did we dedicate the extruders, but we also dedicated the downstream activity so that we were much more efficient. People that used to be responsible for moving things around the plant were redeployed elsewhere in the company

Finally, people were assigned to working value streams rather than being moved around among multiple product lines, so they were able to get really good at making their product as they became more focused on it. The teams were also dedicated with ownership. Teams were assigned to each value stream. Instead of having extruder operators and packaging people we had product leads who owned their equipment and more importantly the process.

The company was able to manage with fewer material handlers, fewer changeovers, faster line speeds and increased production. No production planners and no production books being gathered up since the line leads knew what they were supposed to make since it wasn't changing all of the time.

Large rewinding equipment on the smaller cells that used to be moved in and out of the cell depending upon the open capacity of the extruders were switched to dedicated. Since it was no longer necessary to move these in and out they could be made more substantial and stable. This led to additional innovation that made them work faster.

We were able to cross train to people to run the lines so that we didn't need as much staff. And when the extruders were down, the workers were able to participate in other areas of the operations, such as general clean up and inventory counts.

Often, the type of equipment and your ability to dedicate it can be clouded by the complexity involved in your product offerings. Clearly distinguishing between Quad 1 products and others offers the leverage to identify meaningful opportunities to dedicate equipment.

In another operation, we were able to incorporate mills and drills directly into the assembly cells. Originally the company had work cells for machining and then transferred the machined product over to assembly. This design was based on the generally held belief that machining called for a different skill set than assembly. Obviously this was all done in batch - large runs, large inventory, and large material handling processes.

Implementing the tool of dedicated machining equipment, we purchased smaller mills and incorporated them into the middle of the assembly area so that parts could be machined as needed. Parts were passed one or two at a time to assembly where they were immediately placed into the tools for assembly and then shipment.

Equipment that had historically been broken down and constantly reset was now dedicated to a specific manufacturing process. If we weren't running the job, then the equipment sat idle. While counterintuitive from an operations perspective, this approach proved far more efficient and effective at meeting the needs of our customers.

In this same example, we created value stream owners who could machine, assemble, and package so that employees felt a sense of owner- ship of their line. Breaking down the mentality of machiners vs. assemblers vs. packaging folks took time and some cajoling, but the eventual sense of ownership paid off in terms of productivity and ongoing process improvement ideas from those closest to the process.

With encouragement people take ownership of their area and have the best ideas on how to improve the process.

QUESTIONS

- What resources do you need to provide services/product to your customers?

- Who determines the allocation of these resources for the company?

- Is the allocation of these resources complex or simple?

- Are their frequent quality issues and set-up requirements?

- Does a Quad 1 product or a grouping of Quad 1 products consume over 80% of the resources of any one piece of equipment?

- How does your Quad 2 and Quad 4 product interfere with the production of your Quad 1?

- What would your business look like if you only made your Quad 1 products?

- What variables interfere with your ability to group together products sufficient to dedicate equipment to them?

- Is your work force organized by function or value stream?

CHECKLIST

- For your Quad 1 products do you understand the equipment and processes required to make these?

- Do you have the capacity needs of each of your Quad 1 products by equipment based on their volume?

- Have you systematically gone through your company and allocated product/services to equipment and services?

- Have you reviewed the extra capacity you would have if you no longer have to perform required set-up work?

- Which variables will interfere with your ability to dedicate equipment or personnel?

One At A Time Manufacturing

DESCRIPTION

Setting up your lines/factory/service in such a way that you start, assemble, package and move to a shipping or service area one at a time. The alternative to one at a time is a batch process where you manufacture things in bulk. While the batch approach seems to make intuitive sense (if I am already doing it then I might as well do it 500 times agreement), it is inherently replete with hidden inefficiencies and obstacles.

Below is an illustration of a typical batch vs. one-piece flow. The batch system is set-up typically by function rather than value stream (a value stream encompasses the entire processes or steps required to make a product).

The batch process tends to be capital intensive with the thought being that each process is very specialized and can't be dispersed within the manufacturing lines. Unfortunately, this tends to create fiefdoms within a company, as people don't want to do what is outside their standard work environment.

The batch system tends to add a lot of complexity to an organization. What it does do well is utilize the time invested in setting up an operation. You would typically run a lot of goods through the system once the machinery or equipment is set-up. But you are optimizing the wrong thing. What you want to do is figure out how to eliminate all set-ups. This is best done with dedicated equipment using a one at a time flow.

Exhibit 21
Traditional Batch Production vs Cell In-Line Layout

Traditional Batch Production
(Exponential Number of Transactions)

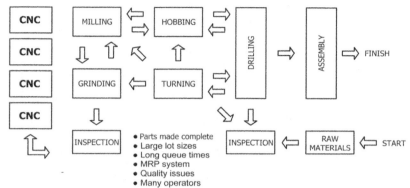

- Parts made complete
- Large lot sizes
- Long queue times
- MRP system
- Quality issues
- Many operators

Cell In-Line Layout - One Value Stream

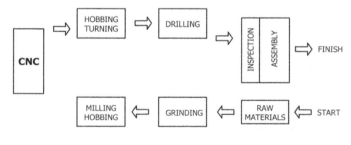

- Automomy, Focus, Ownership
- Small Continuous Runs
- Dedicated Cell Operators

APPLICABLE QUADS

You should try to do this on all of your Quad 1 products and then try to group together your Quad 2 and 4 products into similar manufacturing processes.

This should be done for all of your products/services. It is going to be easier with Quad 1 since you should have the volume to build one piece along with your other toolkit levers.

RELATED TOOLS

You need to do dedicated equipment and in-lining with one at a time. This will make the impact exponential. If you are lacking either of these techniques you will not see the benefit of systems. Employing One-at-a-Time Manufacturing seems very counter intuitive as a manufacturing/service process. The key is that it has to be done in conjunction with the other toolkit items.

Dedicated Equipment

In-Lining Operations

BENEFITS

Ultimately you perform the same number of transactions and steps in either batch or one-at-a-time manufacturing—you just do them in a different order. With one-at-a-time:

- The process is highly visual and intuitive.

- You can watch and time the steps and more easily identify complex processes where you can bring to bear simplification techniques.

- You have an immediate quality check on the product as you go.

- You minimize the amount of misallocation of part quantities (when you have everything except for one part).

- You are immediately putting product on your shelf for shipment.

- Smaller amounts of inventory and people are tied up especially if you need to change direction during the process.

- Forces dedicated equipment—since set-up will be exceptionally unyielding.

You might think that if you reversed this and just did the same step repeatedly (500 times 5) that this would be faster than doing the same steps 5 x 500.

Think of it this way. You are moving product through your inventory rather than your inventory to your product. The One at a Time Manufacturing Process works because laying out the sequential process allows a more visual system, helps fosters the use of dedicate equipment and eliminates material handling/parts flow issues from impacting your assembly line. You need to think through the material handling aspect of the business and this is where the Kanban System and Visual Inventory Management System help you achieve your overall results.

Intellectually this can be a major hurdle for many companies; especially those who have historically manufactured in batch mode. If your company is not already doing this, then you should expect some major resistance.

One at a time production doesn't mean only one person on the line. You can have several people on a line running it in sequence. The key is to have a continual flow with each person working on a part of the process and then moving the product forward towards completion. The best way to teach the benefits of this technique is to use the airplane lesson. The airplane lesson is where you have employees make paper airplanes with some making them in batch and others making them in one-piece flow. You then see the results from the two different manufacturing processes.

There are times when you will have to run a batch process. This is usually done to offset or compensate for a large piece of equipment (a monument) or a situation with excessively high set-up times where the current process dictates the set-up. It just can't be avoided. When this is the case you can help control the flow/impact of this component by isolating its impact through a Kanban Inventory System that removes the process out of the in-lined flow.

One frequently raised objection to this approach is how spikes in demand are managed in a pull through, one-at-a-time, system that is in-lined and set-up using a Kanban System. How do you manage these without being able to bring the entire plant or company to bear on one massive order? Often you will have some ability to see the spikes coming so the first response is to try to reduce a spike by flattening it as much as possible. This might involve calling customers and asking if they might accept two shipments. You could also request a larger lead-time for spikes outside of your kanban quantities.

The advantage of having dedicated lines and cells is that you can isolate the spikes from the rest of your business and allow these to keep running smoothly; thus, avoiding spillage into your other lines. It keeps the chaos contained so the rest of the business can keep running. This is critical since it allows you to focus on that part of your business that is being disruptive, but do so in a manner that is contained and controlled. You then allow the rest of your business to continue to run unimpeded.

EXAMPLES

Let's walk through a simple, home example to see how batch vs. one-at-a-time processes differ.

Suppose you want to bake 100 cakes in one batch. To start, you must get 100 bowls and lay them out. This implies that you need a bigger kitchen and a correspondingly larger capital investment. While your bowls are sitting there you need to go and procure one hundred pounds of flour. This is a lot of flour. If you buy it in 25 pound bags, the cost per pound will come down. On the other hand, you may now need a larger storage room next to your new big kitchen and a hand truck to move the bags of flour from the storage room to the waiting bowls. Does the money you save buying one hundred pounds at a time offset the investment cost of a storage room and the expense of a new hand truck?

Once you have flour in your 100 bowls you need to break 200 eggs; two into each bowl. Unfortunately, as you're moving the eggs from the new walk-in refrigerator you invested in, you drop a dozen on the kitchen floor. You'll probably want to return the six pounds of flour and half-dozen bowls you now don't need to storage so that you don't lose them. Meanwhile, you also need to clean up the mess from the dozen eggs you dropped. You may also start to worry about whether the remaining eggs are becoming little bacteria factories while all of this unplanned work is taking place. Next thing you know, you've hired two assistants to spread the workload in the kitchen, and a bookkeeper to track and manage your perishable raw materials inventory.

Choosing to bake 100 cakes in a single batch necessarily complicates the production process. It entails additional capital investment, equipment, and staffing to accommodate larger production runs.

How long will it take from the start of the process to the end before you obtain your first cake?

What changes would you make if you were to inline with dedicated equipment and a one-piece flow? Perhaps you set up a bank of ovens at one end of a smaller kitchen and dedicate one table to putting flour in the bowl and a second table to mixing in the egg. Put the bowl in the next available oven as soon as the cake you put in that oven twenty minutes ago finishes baking. Deliver that cake to an eagerly waiting customer and your new one-at-a-time, continual flow process can be creating cash flow for your business twenty minutes after you open in the morning.

The inefficiencies in large batch runs need to be compared to the benefits of the process flow when things are done inline and one-at-a-time. However, operations textbooks continue to discuss manufacturing as if batch processes were always the best way.

At MIP we used to make sealing tools in batches of 500 at a time (Exhibit 22). We would pull all of the parts from inventory, place the parts in large trays, bring the loaded trays over to a master assembly area, and then assemble the tools. Often we would find that we only had 498 of a part or 501 of another. This meant someone would have to go back to the stock area and find the correct part or put away the excess parts that we weren't able to use.

We spent a lot of time trying to match up part pulls with tool assembly runs. It always seemed to be the last item on the bill of material where we had picked 498 or 501 parts. When the parts were being returned to stock they would sometimes be put back in the wrong bin especially as some parts looked nearly identical to other parts.

Exhibit 22
Assembling Tools in Batches at MIP

We were constantly re-staging work because of our batch manufacturing bias. This bias created other problems as well. If we assembled something wrong, then every single tool in the batch might be wrong. Even inspecting the first tool completed could result in dozens of incorrectly assembled tools. This truly was an expensive proposition.

At the time we believed this was the most efficient way of assembling. Who could possibly compete with us making 500 of these tools at a time? We were intensely skeptical that we would find a one-piece flow more efficient than a 500 tool build, but opted to run the experiment.

A dedicated work area was assigned for the assembly of these products. Bins for the various components were set-up and color coded to eliminate mistakes. An assembly slider device was made so that you could walk the tool down the assembly line putting on the correct pieces and then moving forward. We then started to clock the time each step took. Tool Balancers were put in place with pneumatic tighteners. As we focused on solving specific manufacturing problems, we were able to make products faster one at a time rather than in batch. After working with the assembly folks we reached the point where we could assemble a unit in less than 2 minutes. With 2400 minutes in a 40-hour week, one person could manufacture 1200 units a week. But even as one of our best selling products, we were only selling 400 a week. One third of one assembly worker's time met the demand for one of our leading products.

We would never have discovered this without breaking the assembly process down into its simplest steps and learning how to simplify and streamline each step.

QUESTIONS

- Is your facility set-up by function or value stream?

- What are the primary obstacles to going to a one-piece flow?

- What types of process or services have complicated set-ups or require several of the various SKU's be run through them?

- Is the inflow of raw material easy and accessible? Are the items easy to move to finished goods?

- Do you have a lot of material handlers moving items around the company?

- Is the production process and finished goods demand visual?

CHECKLIST

- Have your determined your top value streams in your Quad 1?

- Have you laid out the process for the assembly/service in such way that you are in-lined with dedicated equipment creating one-at-a-time production flow?

- Are there shared pieces of equipment that would interfere with your processes?

- Have you done the throughput calculations on how long it will take someone to do the assembly at your annual volume? If this requires more than one person have you balanced your line so that these people are working together to create the flow?

Decentralized Cell Leads: Autonomy, Ownership and Empowerment

DESCRIPTION

Develop systems that hold individuals responsible for the work they perform by assigning them to a cell or value stream. These individuals need the tools, equipment, and materials needed to get the job done and make them accountable. You want to make the process visual so that all parties know their goals and how they are performing. This is all about assigning ownership, accountability, and empowerment around a value stream.

In larger organizations, it is especially critical to allow cell leaders to manage and run the area they control. By pushing the responsibility down to the value stream/cell levels you hold people accountable for their work and empower them to improve their area. This is critical as the size and volume of the business grows.

The key is being able to break down the Quad 1 value stream into an in-lined process with dedicated equipment and visual inventory and then task an individual/group with managing this cell.

To facilitate autonomy:

- Train cell leads in Kanban Systems so they understand the general flow of the system, the management of their work orders, and the potential efficiency of their line.

- Make cell leads fully accountable for their value stream and the management of their area. This includes basic 5S principles and visual management.

- Hold cell lead accountable for the quality of inbound parts and materials as well as finished goods produced.

- Have cell lead put away the parts for their area. This insures that they will know the inventory situation for their cell.

- Task the team as a whole on the improvement of their cell.

Below is the list of structural items you can perform in your company to help create the cell leadership. This is a bottom up approach where management needs to turn over the running of the cells to the cell leaders. Standard work is often a major trigger within a lean organization. However most efforts with standard work tend to be management with stopwatches trying to control employee behavior rather the employee involvement trying to simplify tasks.

Exhibit 23
Cell Leadership Expectations

Ownership/Autonomy

- This is your area to maintain, understand, and enforce the systems.
- You need to keep it running and improve it.
- Maintain equipment and supplies.
- Visual board to communicate issues.
- You have the tools, equipment, and information to run your area.

Accountability

- Maintain the finished goods.
- Maintain Kanban System.
- Maintain 5S.
- Inform management of problems, opportunities, and solutions.
- Focus on Quality.
- Hold other people in the company responsible for their part of the system.

Empowerment

- You decide what to make.
- You can change and rearrange your cell.
- You can get the tools you need to run your cell.
- You can work with management to isolate problems and require that they be fixed.
- You can bring up difficult work and then task the team with solving it.

Use the board to post information.

Visual Flag if you are having production, QC, or any other problem requiring management attention. This is a self-reporting system. You must notify management if you are not meeting production levels.

APPLICABLE QUADS

This system should be set up across all the Quads. But it is most effective in Quad 1 where the volume exists to create continual flow through the company.

RELATED TOOLS

This system works the best when you bring all of the prior elements to bear into the process.

In-Lining Operations

Dedicated Equipment

One At A Time Manufacturing

Kanban—Inventory Management Systems

BENEFITS

You create accountability, empowerment, and ownership. This will make employees feel more like an owner of the process rather than just a passive participant in the process. It becomes their responsibility to keep product flowing rather than the just the management's

In addition, it allows your floor supervisor to be more of a manager. Your employees can then focus on the continual improvement process and implementing the changes needed to get the efficiencies out of the process.

This can be an enormous cultural shift in a company. You are empowering people on the floor to take responsibility within their area, come up with improvement ideas, and be responsible for their own destiny. The key in this tool is that people feel they have the ability and authority to make change.

Successfully creating a real sense of ownership can generate the fastest, most effective change in a company. A lot of it is strictly a numbers game – you either have a hand full of management folks working to implement change or you have your entire shop floor who know and understand the process better than the management.

While Kaizens can be an effective change methodology often it turns into an exercise of management telling employees what to do even though this is contrary to general premise of Kaizens. With employee value stream ownership, efficiencies and ideas appear, quality goes up and employees are encouraged to be involved. This is a continual process of improvement, not a one-week event. This creates an environment that fosters this sense of ownership. It demands that real power and authority be pushed down to the plant floor level.

People on the plant floor won't accept this power and authority if they believe that efficiencies and improvements only put their hours or jobs at risk. This is a critical condition for this process to be successful. If employees feel that the changes they implement result in fewer of them or fewer hours then they will quietly not participate. If you believe that you are overstaffed relative to expected demands, you want to make cutbacks once and deeply enough for the workforce that remains to believe your assurances that their jobs remain secure. You don't want folks thinking that 80/20 thinking is about job elimination. While this can occur, the driving force is simplification. Employee engagement and participation in the process is essential.

EXAMPLES

This was recently accomplished in a large, highly structured organization with a deep bill of material. The company had a history of strict management and main office control. Cells had been successfully in-lined, but production flow was still being dictated by a planner, inventory was being managed by the computer programs, and floor personnel did what they were told each day. Everyone was afraid of doing anything outside of what they were told. It was not a particularly pleasant work environment especially since people felt like they weren't being successful. There had been a series of layoffs and management changes over the years. The company was losing money and the frequency of parts shortages was excessive. The parts order process was controlled by the front office and the plant works just accepted the fact that their lines were often shutdown due to parts shortages

Empowering employees took time. Cell leaders were assigned and trained in lean manufacturing practices through a monthly meeting. Production planning was pushed down to the plant floor for each value stream. Inventory was placed in a very visual Kanban system and cell leaders were given control over it.

It took six months for people to become fully engaged and start to participate in the new system. Daily production cadence became consistent. Parts shortages evaporated and systems to streamline operations were developed by the cell leads themselves. The company was able to successfully absorb a 15% decrease in the work force including the production planner and one purchasing agent and then quickly started turning a profit.

QUESTIONS

- Is production planning centralized or decentralized?

- Do you have a large planning department?

- Is there a leader held accountable for each value stream.

- Are there financial awards for the performance of the value stream?

- Are the metrics for each value stream posted and kept up by the cell leader?

- Do the designated Cell Leaders make more money because of their role?

- Is the system visual on a daily basis so that the Cell Leaders know how they are doing, what they need to make and the inventory situation?

- Are successes by the line leads celebrated?

- Is there a concerted effort to train and empower the line leads?

- Are the line leads empowered to change flow, inventory placement, request dedicated tools and create their ideal workflow in conjunction with management?

CHECKLIST

- Have you broken your Quad 1 workflow into individually identified workflows?

- Are the value streams autonomous enough to hold folks accountable for their work?

- Do the cell leaders have control over everything they do so they are truly empowered to run their areas or do they have to wait for information or inventory from another area?

- Have you made the finished goods situation visual so that the cell leader has the capability of making the correct decision on what to make?

- Do cell leads have the information and resources they need to run their area?

- Has management stepped away enough to let the cells leaders run their area?

Daily Value Stream Walks (Gemba Walks)

DESCRIPTION

Daily management walks through the value stream of the company. This should start with the receiving area continue through the production floor to shipping and purchasing. If you are a service business you would start with the supplies you need to service your customer. This process is most effective in the operational/service part of the business and needs to be done daily. You need to include customer service and sales in the walk as well. This daily walk, often referred to as a Gemba walk (from the Japanese word "Gemba," meaning "real place"), is one of the strongest ways to establish a regular daily cadence in your manufacturing/service operation.

At the start of the day, gather in the shipping department as out-going orders are being prepared. Include your core functional leaders of the company since they are key drivers in decision-making processes. The intention is not to add another meeting to everyone's workload. It is to eliminate meetings by having this be the primary point of daily communication. Work your way through the entire organization seeing that everything is operating properly and objectives are being met. The key to a successful Gemba walk is a production process that is visual and contains the information you need to readily access what is going on. Make certain that each area has a board visibly displaying the metrics and statistics pertinent to the value stream. If you don't know where to start, then start with a Safety, Quality, Delivery, Cost (SQDC) board. There are plenty of sources online that show a sample standard SQDC board.

This daily review works under the assumption that if you deal with your issues daily then the weeks, months, and years will take care of themselves. You can easily see what is working and what is not working. The daily nature of it means you have the ability to respond immediately. If all is well, move on. If something is wrong, everyone can observe the exception from the same vantage point and problem solve on the spot. The key is to mark the problem on the board, assign someone who is responsible for it and then have that person circle back later in the day and write down what they did to solve it. In one operation where we had problems with items being processed through receiving we set up a penalty box and placed this in the middle of our walk. Any time something was older than 2 days it was moved into the box. This way it was exceptionally visible when an item sat for longer than a day or so. Consequently, it was immediately dealt with. After about 3 weeks of this process the penalty box remained empty and the receiving issue was resolved.

The Gemba walk sends a clear message to the plant floor that the functional leaders are vested in the entire operation and understand the daily issues. Try to keep a certain pace to these walks each day. Learn to listen and allow cross-functional team members to offer suggestions or ideas on how to solve various problems or issues. Use the five why technique (ask "Why?" five times to get to the root cause of a problem and identify a solution). Visual boards need to be posted outside of each value stream and these need to be the focus of discussions.

Toward the end of each day the shipping manager, customer service manager and operations manager should meet again. The objective is to review pending critical orders, confirm that orders shipped without incident, identify what materials have been received, and understand what is expected tomorrow. This should be a short, five-minute discussion, always in the area where the product is being made or shipped.

APPLICABLE QUADS

All Quads will benefit from this. The Gemba walk is critical to the successful running of a lean organization. Obviously the daily cadence impacts Quad 1 products the most.

RELATED TOOLS

Visual Management and line lead management are critical to the success of this process. Kanban Inventory systems with pending orders post-ed visually are also needed.

Decentralized Cell Leads: Autonomy, Ownership and Empowerment

Kanban—Inventory Management Systems

BENEFITS

This is one of the strongest management tools in our toolkit. The daily walk has the power to drive a business forward through improved communication and problem solving.

Cell leads maintain visual production boards that communicate what is going on in their cell. You might include the pending schedule, labor issues, production efficiencies, inventory issues, quality issues, and any other issue that might merit management attention as possible metrics.

It needs to be done every single day. Your employees will be testing your commitment to the process. On a brisk pace it should take no longer than 20-30 minutes. In the beginning, it will seem a bit awkward and it might take a while to find its cadence, but if you are persistent then you will get there. The key is that your cell leaders learn that issues that are raised during the Gemba Walk are addressed.

EXAMPLES

The daily operational walks were transformative in a business we recently worked with, which was replete with operational issues. The daily operations meetings were occurring in the operational conference room. The typical discussion involved people trying to decide what they could make based on parts availability and what parts they needed to chase. The planning person running the meeting was always the hero because he controlled all of the information on pending orders and shipments. He would often pull a surprise delivery or new important information out during the meeting to show how he had helped the group as a whole. He also provided the most resistance to the process as it was pushed out onto the plant floor.

We eliminated this meeting and replaced it with an early morning walk of the facility. The metrics boards that were placed in front of each line started to evolve to display the information that we needed to quickly access the health of each line. Most of this was standard SQDC material.

In the beginning the boards were full of parts issues, but slowly these got addressed through a successful Kanban System. As the parts started to come in the operating efficiency went up and we started to get a strong flow going within each cell. When there was an issue that was going to shut down a line, then it would be addressed immediately. After 3 to 4 months the lines were never actually shut down. It took a while to break old habits. Often cell leaders tried to control the Kanban cards rather than turning them in.

Before long there was a steady cadence established within each line. The efficiency of each line increased dramatically and On-Time Delivery increased to high 90s percentages.

QUESTIONS

- Can you walk your company and know its general health within 20-30 minutes?

- Do your daily management meetings happen inside a conference room?

- Do your supervisors and managers spend most of their time in front of a computer screen and get their information from computer reports?

- Do segments of your business get shut down because of unexpected issues?

- Is the communication from the floor up to upper management clear and daily?

CHECKLIST

- Is the information you need to run your business visually posted within each cell?

- Are you walking your entire value stream every single day and engaging a line lead to discuss what is going on in their area?

- Do you assign responsibility as you go?

- Do your Cell Leaders know their pending production requirements?

- Are people held responsible to follow up and resolve issues?

- Do you have owners of each value stream?

- Are the general manager/operational leaders of the business participating when they are in town on these walks?

- Are problems on the boards assigned to the functional leads and do people solve the problems that are posted?

CHAPTER 10
INVENTORY CONTROL AND
IMPROVEMENT TECHNIQUES

Kanban—Inventory Management Systems

DESCRIPTION—FINISHED GOODS AND WORK IN PROCESS

Kanban is a system for managing inventory visually. Typically, an inventory of parts or work in process (WIP) inventory is divided equally between two bins. Sometimes, a 3, 4, or 5 bin system may be more appropriate. The concept is that you work out of one bin while the empty bin triggers a reorder of items. Calculating the bin quantities correctly (see Appendix 3 for an example of the calculations) greatly simplifies inventory management while keeping the investment in inventory acceptably low. Differences in material handling needs, high value parts, or vendor price breaks can make accommodations in the approach necessary. However, the goal of keeping a constant supply of parts while lowering inventory amounts remains the same. A good Kanban System will always drive your inventory investment lower. This will improve your return on invested capital by decreasing the amount of money required for your business.

Through this system, the flow of product in and out of the company can remain constant. The relationship between inventory usage, lead time, and the variability of factors that affect your lead time will determine your inventory quantity.

Exhibit 24
Kanban Two Bin System

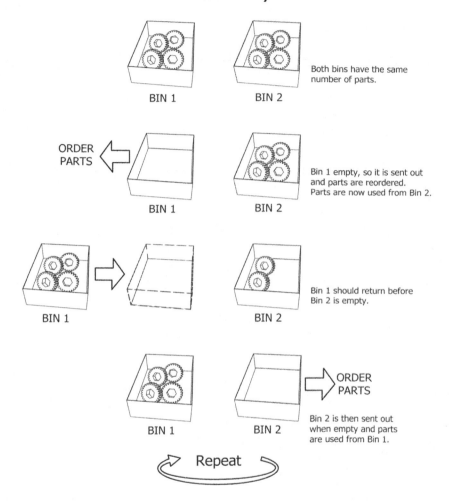

Both bins have the same number of parts.

BIN 1   BIN 2

ORDER PARTS

Bin 1 empty, so it is sent out and parts are reordered. Parts are now used from Bin 2.

BIN 1   BIN 2

Bin 1 should return before Bin 2 is empty.

BIN 1   BIN 2

ORDER PARTS

Bin 2 is then sent out when empty and parts are used from Bin 1.

BIN 1   BIN 2

Repeat

INVENTORY CONTROL TECHNIQUES

Inventory in your company should be classified into one of four categories: finished goods, WIP, raw materials, and C-Class. All of these should be managed using a Kanban approach; however, the approach tends to vary slightly between categories. Each plays a role in the overall efficient management of the production system.

Inventory acts as buffers within your organization to allow each facet to operate independently so you can run each area in the most efficient manner.

Randomness in your business will occur whether this is from your vendors or customers. This randomness can be extremely expensive when it is shutting down a production area due to lack of parts or is causing a break in the system to accommodate a spike in demand.

Inventory levels must be large enough to buffer the overall operating system from non-performing vendors or random acts impacting your supply of parts. The better control you have over your vendors the better you can control the randomness and their ability to respond to it.

In addition, you are going to have variation in customer demand, but you want to carry enough inventory to buffer your operations/service side from this variation so that they can operate in the most efficient manner within this sphere. You also want to carry enough finished goods so that the shipping department can easily ship and pull orders. The key is to manage this so that each element of your company can function the most efficiently within their area while carrying as little inventory as possible.

In effect, inventory serves as shock absorbers to smooth out the bumps in various areas of the system. As with shock absorbers, you don't want to damage the system by ignoring them. At the same time, you want to be able to sense and handle the curves in road as they occur.

Generally, **finished goods inventory** should be able to handle two weeks worth of demand at any one time. Obviously, you need to review the overall demand cadence to make certain that you won't run out of inventory. Usually you can examine this with what is called a backwash analysis. You take the expected inventory levels, run them back over the order demand for the last six months, and see how many times you actually exhaust your stock.

Standard **WIP inventory** contains items that are critical for your business. They are inventory items of high value that can't be procured or made quickly. These are the items to monitor carefully to ensure a constant, controlled flow of inventory.

Raw Material inventory is especially conducive to Kanban management. It's generally better to institute after you have made a push to consolidate the number of SKU's in a line simplification effort. In one case, we had a business with three different types of steel. It was an easy decision to go to one type of steel since with the combined volume we could go to the highest grade at pretty much the same cost.

An important factor in all of this is the panic time it takes to manufacture a part. For instance, something that is made on a CNC machine using common steel without heat treatment can usually be delivered in a day if needed; whereas an investment casting part may take up to 4 weeks from start to finish. Specialized medicines could be another example of something that can't be produced in a single day. For parts with longer lead times, such as investment casting parts, you should keep larger quantities in your inventory. You can't just develop your Kanban Quantities on a spreadsheet. You need to bring some experience and expertise into the process.

Items that have a high QC requirement and are subject to rejection may also need a higher buffer stock.

C Class inventory consists of items you want to have physically on hand, are typically of low value, and can be obtained relatively easy. The most obvious example is fasteners. Machine screws, for example, are better to simply expense rather than add the transaction and complexity overhead of receiving and accounting for these items in and out of inventory. The simplicity of keeping a quarter's worth of usage on the production floor as the relevant Kanban quantity easily offsets the small cost of the materials themselves. The intention with C class is to strip out the 20/80 of the transactions that tend to distract from focusing on what is important.

APPLICABLE QUADS

Kanbans should be set-up throughout your facility and in every part of the company. It is a min/max system with your one Kanban being your minimum and two kanbans being your max. Obviously the Quad 1 products are the most important but the inability to manufacture product in a Quad 2 group can be just as impactful or distracting to an important customer.

Setting up your Quad 4 on Kanban should only be done after you have completed your line simplification process and thought through what you need. In some cases you may develop a separate system to manage the Quad 4 because it may not lend itself to small, frequent delivery of parts/sales. The management of the Quad 4 is inherently more complicated than the management of your Quad 1.

RELATED TOOLS

Kanbans work best with Visual Management because if the Kanban System is set-up properly you can directly observe inventory status during your Gemba walk.

Decentralized Cell Leads are also critical because you want to task the cell lead with running their area and reporting any looming shortages. The one at a time manufacturing flow is critical because things come through system in a steady, incremental fashion. A lean company works best when you are able to get to small, frequent output and small frequent input. Think of the flow of water rather than the flow of boulders.

Visual Systems

Decentralized Leads: Autonomy, Ownership and Empowerment

One At A Time Manufacturing

Daily Value Stream Walks: (Gemba Walks)

BENEFITS

You will have inventory to sell to your customers. Your plant will run more effectively. Forget all of the other lean stuff. The most inefficient thing you can do in your business is to not have the parts or finished goods you need to run effectively.

It doesn't mean to over buy – when you over buy it becomes even harder to manage your inventory. It means setting up the systems so that you have the proper amount of inventory to operate as buffer stock between functional areas of your company without over purchasing. The objective here is to maximize the return on invested capital. Inventory tends to be among the largest items on the balance sheet.

At the end of this Kanban Process – most companies end up with two weeks of finished goods, two weeks of assembly parts, two weeks of raw material. The overall inventory of the company is 6 weeks on hand with the lowest conceivable turn ratio of 8 times. However, inventory turns are often much higher because you rarely hit full capacity on all the Kanbans. This tends to be the starting point and as you fine-tune the process you get to even better numbers.

Could you imagine Starbucks running out of cups? The entire store would shut down. However, this happens all of the time in complex manufacturing environments.

There is absolutely no excuse for this in an organization. It is just too costly. Over purchasing inventory adds complexity to the organization. It also uses up the inventory of capital that allows the business to expand. The most clairvoyant, efficient inventory management system is a lean system.

The most important thing to do is calculate Kanban Quantities correctly. In the beginning err on the side of too much inventory but think through the process so you can down scale easily as you go forward. We are suggesting that you go for a triple or ground-rule double rather than a home run when you first set-up the Kanban System.

The easiest and least risky place to have safety stock is in your finished goods. Downsizing your finished goods tends to be easy with the change of one placard rather than a lot of bins.

The second most important thing is the discipline on the Kanban. This needs to be enforced first through education and observation. It will take enforcement. Most people working on the production floor will not trust Kanban at the outset. You can expect to find people hiding cards in their desks, turning cards in early because they are worried about running out of stock, and generally diluting the potential of Kanban out of fear.

Kanban Rules are SIMPLE:

1. LINE PERSONNEL – Bin is empty – turn in re-order trigger.

2. PURCHASING-ORDERING – Receive Trigger – Order Part.

3. RECEIVING – Monitor Old Cards and Match up Cards with Parts.

Typically there are a lot of old habits to break.

Kanban cards are generally simple as the following example illustrates.

Exhibit 25
Sample Kanban Card

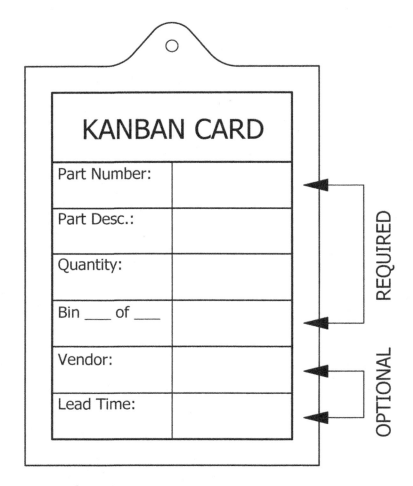

- Simple
- Highly visual
- Color coded by value stream

Kanbans can be used to effectively drive behavior. Think through the situation understanding the complexities of a business and then figure a way through them. Other issues you encounter often deal with size, distance, and weight.

EXAMPLES

In one transformation we helped set-up they had two significant issues driving operations. The first problem was that there were families of products that required similar tooling and had to be run together as a whole. The second issue was that you had a defined production process that once you were in a family you needed to run the entire family filling all of the inventory needs for that family. Once in a family, it might take 3-4 days to run through the rest of the family.

Set-ups were complicated often required the machine to be down for several hours while changing over the raw material mix. The first approach was to try to consolidate the raw material to simplify the conversion process.

The planner had been trying to manage all of this complexity to minimize inventory, minimize changeover and meet customer's demand. They had not done particularly well with the planner requiring frequent breaks in the runs to fulfill orders for various customers resulting in an inefficient production process.

The interesting part of solving this was that we were able to use the Kanban System to drive the desired behavior on the plant floor. We set up a visual board with three Kanban buckets. We wanted the SKU's from Quad 1 to always be the trigger for the production cycle within the family. They had the volume and critical mass to justify a change over. So we set these up on standard two Kanban bins, the Quad 2 products, we set-up on a three Kanban system with larger volumes and, for the small Quad 4 products, we set up on a six-month supply.

As the operator rotated through this system then they would build up their cards and once they had a Quad 1 card then they would start to work the family into the production cycle looking for opportunities to manage the family into the run.

By varying the Kanban sizes by Quad – we were able to make certain the company had enough critical mass to run a family efficiently and justify a set-up change over, but avoiding running a family because we were out of the Quad 2 and 4 SKUs.

We also added a couple of basic rules, if the number of cards from Quad 1 and Quad 2 items built up to a certain level then this family would be moved up into the production run. If a Quad 1 Kanban ran out of stock then the entire family would be run next. Other than these two rules, the operator was allowed to manage his/her production run. This was all made very visual with the Quad 1 products being colored one way and the other cards being colored another way. As the cards were received, they were placed into the production rack so you could see the cards grouped by family with a visual trigger showing that the family had crossed over into the production needed range.

QUESTIONS

- What is your inventory turn?

- Do you frequently run out of parts?

- Is your inventory run from the plant floor through a visual system or via a computer program?

- How complicated are your bills of materials?

- Do you spend an excessive amount of time on non-critical items?

- Is your inventory visual?

- Are you able to meet your customer's demand via your finished goods?

CHECKLIST

- Need to make the decision to run your business via Kanban.

- Have you dumped your inventory into a spreadsheet and performed the proper calculations.

- Who in the organization will manage the transition to Kanban? This is complicated and needs someone's focus.

- Have you thought about your Kanban Triggers – how will they be displayed on the product, Who will collect these and place the orders, how will the inbound inventory be retagged as it comes back into place?

- Do you have any visual issues, storage issues, or material-handling issues?

- Who in the organization will be responsibility for managing high value, non-C class inventory to make certain as you start the new process you don't miss anything critical.

- Have you set-up your Kanban System Visual.

- Do your employees understand the process?

- Have you pushed the responsibility down far enough into the organization?

Raw Material Kanban

DESCRIPTION RAW MATERIAL AND WIP INVENTORY

The inflow of raw materials in your company is one of the critical aspects to successfully running a business. When you run out of raw material, you have a huge disruption to your manufacturing process. This is exceptionally expensive. Having too much raw material inventory is also expensive and tends to add an enormous amount of complexity to a business.

However, having someone in the management team act as "planner" trying to forecast the future is particularly difficult and tends to be replete with error, especially if you have a lot of randomness to your customer's ordering pattern. We have yet to find any company that doesn't think of their orders as being sporadic and unpredictable.

A Raw Material Kanban system works on a trigger system with two Kanbans set-up to manage your incoming material. Most people have trouble determining where to start. How do we set up a raw material Kanban? The answer tends to hinge significantly on your particular business but is nonetheless done along the same lines as for finished goods. There are some simple methodologies to calculate them – but you need to heavily involve your plant personnel and your purchasing department. If you do it strictly by a mathematical formula, then the system won't work. However, you need the formula in order to get started.

Appendix 3 contains formulas to calculate Kanban sizes. This gives you a starting point for discussion.

Not having the right quantity in your Kanbans will collapse your system and discourage people from using it. Their first reaction to any problem will be to go back to the old way of doing stuff. If you set the quantity too low then you run the risk of running out of the raw material. It's analogous to starting a train. Once a train is started it runs fast, but getting all of the boxcars running at the same speed in the same direction takes a lot of work.

A Kanban System is the most efficient way to manufacture product, but if it gets off track, then you do need to go back and reset it. Getting the train started again can be problematic.

APPLICABLE QUADS

Raw Material Kanbans are going to be impact directly your Quad 1 products. These are the items you want to set-up and have run through your company almost without interference on a daily basis.

If your Quad 2 and 4 products tend to be spiky with an inconsistent demand pattern you either develop a system to pull inventory in quickly, or pay a little more attention to this part of your business and run larger quantities. Often you will find that 80/20 works in these Quads as well and that Quad 2 and Quad 4 also have a couple of driver products.

RELATED TOOLS

Rolling Purchase Order System (RPOS), Vendor Consolidation, and Line Leads: Autonomy and Decentralization are each critical to driving down your inventory. It is the combination of these three techniques that will drive down inventory significantly.

Rolling Purchase Order System (RPOS)

Vendor Consolidation

Decentralized Leads: Autonomy, Ownership and Empowerment

BENEFITS

Efficient production.

You would prefer 3 things from your vendors: Delivery, Quality and Price.

When you are always focused on delivery then this is all you will discuss with your vendors.

EXAMPLES

Recently we transformed a company with a very high level bill of material that was a complex assembly system. The company was constantly being run out of parts and the efficiency in the assembly area was dismal. They were basically "Ferrying" the production process and it had been going on so long that people had come to expect this as a way of life.

"Ferrying" is our term for running from one production area to another production area utilizing your personnel to make as much of anything because you have the parts and then running back to the other area and making product because the parts have become available. We call it "Ferrying" because folks are running from one side of the ferry to the other side to avoid having the ferry sink, but at the same time they are creating the next tilt. Remember small, incremental flow is the best way to run a company.

To get the entire business to a steady state—Kanban on the raw material was implemented with a visual board outside of each line. The board contained the Kanban cardholder and then an emergency short list. The cards were collected and the orders placed and then anything that would shut the line down within 48 hours was posted. The sourcing people would then track down these parts.

We also posted the weeks production above the board (incremental step) so that the cell leaders could see what they needed to make for the next couple days. This allowed them to check their inventory and actually plan.

In the beginning when we started the process we had to have several meetings with the line leads. It took time to get them on board and to believe in the system. Typical problems were folks posting things that they didn't need within 48 hours since they were so used to running out of inventory and then not turning in the Kanban Cards trying to help manage the inventory themselves. We also had problems with purchasing people keeping the cards and not placing orders immediately.

It took about 4 months, but we were able to eliminate these issues. When we left the business unit we were running between 96% to 99% on-time delivery, up from the mid-80s when we began.

This process was successful because we brought in the discipline into the process and worked to educate the people involved in the general expectations.

QUESTIONS

- Does your company ever get shut down based on parts supply?

- Are you turning your inventory over 12 times per year?

- What is the dispersion of you inventory turn by part?

- How do you manage part shortages within your organization?

- Do you have a steady flow of product coming out of each cell?

CHECKLIST

- Have you set up your top 80/20 Vendors?

- Are your Kanban Cards visual and contain the proper information?

- Are your bins visual so you can walk your plant floor and see when you are empty?

- Have you set up a system to deal with items that are going to shut down your line?

C-Class Inventory: 80/20 Thinking and Inventory

DESCRIPTION

You should set up two main types of WIP Kanban Classifications - regular inventory and C-class. The regular inventory represents anything above a pre-set level of cost that is counted and managed with a company. Regular Inventory tends to be tracked and brought onto the books and then expensed as they are used. There is a cutoff point for items that need to be recorded on the books and their value recognized by the company for tax purposes. This regular inventory is counted and controlled when it is brought into the company.

"C" class inventory items are not recorded on the books as inventory. They are expensed as received. This eliminates a tremendous amount of transactions in a company. C-class items are inexpensive, readily available from outside parties and have short lead times for manufacturing.

Adopting a quarterly Kanban quantity is preferred for C-class items, as it can significantly reduce the amount of material handling in the company. If you lose a couple of parts from time to time the cost is nothing in comparison to the simplification that is brought into the company. Obviously you do some spot counts from time to time to look for vendors that might be mistaken in their counts. Through your vendor reduction program (discussed later in this section) you will end up discouraging any behavior that might jeopardize the relationship.

Another system that is even easier is to have your vendors come in and actually fill your C-class products in a specific area or within your cell. The vendors will then invoice you for the product. This is typically a vendor managed inventory (VMI) system. For a number of companies, this expensing of C-class represents the simplest method. At one business unit, this methodology changed our inventory counting process from a dreaded two-day affair to a much simpler four-hour task.

A lot of folks like to have goods placed on consignment on their floor and are invoiced for them as they are used. This system can work to reduce your inventory—but it adds some complexity to the company. Given proper inventory control you should be able to get your turns to a level where the consignment benefit is nominal.

One regularly voiced objection to this process is that expensing C-class items "will harm our income statement because we will have to recognize the expense immediately and income will become more erratic."

There is some theoretical truth to this; however, in practice the pattern in every company is to raise the issue, object vehemently, make the change, and discover it to be a non-issue. Expensing C-class parts has a one-time impact but given a broad enough base and randomness in the business the financial impact proves to be minimal.

APPLICABLE QUADS

Primarily Quad 1 for large volume products.

RELATED TOOLS

Vendor Consolidation

Decentralized Leads: Autonomy, Ownership and Empowerment

BENEFITS

In most cases, you should be able to strip out 30 to 50% of your transactions in your company and just create a steady stream of products coming into the business. This allows you to focus on the most important aspect of your business, which is your core inventory.

EXAMPLES

In one company there was a full time inventory counter who did nothing all day except count inventory. The expense from this activity was very high and often unproductive. By using the C-class process we were able to reduce the number of inventory items that were counted to several hundred, which was then turned over to the cell leads to do once a week.

The cell leads were much more effective at counting the inventory since they knew where the inventory was and how best to count it. They also had a vested interest in making certain the inventory was correct.

QUESTIONS

- Do you have a lot of miscellaneous, inexpensive parts within your company?

- How difficult is it to procure these parts?

- How expensive are these parts?

CHECKLIST

- Isolated the parts that you want to C-class?

- Set up a visual system to trigger their reorder?

- Properly calculated their quantities to insure continued supply?

- Worked with vendors to set this up?

- Determined the expense to converting your existing inventory over to C-class?

- What are your C class items? For most manufacturing companies it is fasteners, packaging and labels. For Starbucks, it might be napkins and stirrers, for a hospital it might be gloves, clean up rags and tape.

- When you go C class you are going to have to write-off existing inventory levels within your company. Do you have the ability to absorb this write-off?

Consolidating Raw Material

DESCRIPTION

One area where you can achieve considerable improvement in your operations is the consolidation of your raw materials. This consolidation allows the processing and flow of products to improve, strips out complexity and allows you to streamline your operations. In this process you may need to think a bit outside the box in order to think inside the box. It is imperative that you challenge yourself and the company to see what you can do to consolidate your raw material.

APPLICABLE QUADS

This would be a focus across the company. You want to understand what raw materials you need for your Quad 1, but also understand the complexity that is brought into your business by non-core raw materials. Any Quad 2 or Quad 4 product that requires additional raw material SKU's needs to be scrutinized for why you need to carry these products.

RELATED TOOLS

This works in conjunction with Vendor Consolidation and the Rolling Purchase Order System and the visual management of Raw Material Kanbans.

Rolling Purchase Order System (RPOS)

Vendor Consolidation

Raw Material Kanban

BENEFITS

Simplification of processes through out the organization. When you have less variability running through you company you can have fewer change-overs, it is easier to group jobs together, and the knowledge required to run work in the company is less since you are working with fewer materials. The other key is that you will be able to carry lower inventory. There is an inherent amount of randomness in any business, but when you take three SKUs and lump them into one SKU then you can offset the randomness and take the average of the three. This means you can carry less stock since the randomness in one group of product will offset the randomness in the other group of product.

Also, as you consolidate raw material, visual systems and purchasing opportunities will become more readily apparent. It is much easier to set up a visual system with 20 items of raw material than it is with 100. While you might pay a bit more for the material there is an enormous amount of simplification that occurs.

EXAMPLES

In one company we transformed we discovered that they were using three different types of steel each requiring different heat treatment and specifications. The original intent was to match steel purchases to the properties of the steel in order to drive down costs. What we found was that we could consolidate all of the purchases into better quality steel, but by purchasing this steel in bulk we could obtain it from the mill at a much

115

lower price. This eliminated an enormous amount of confusion on the internal transactions that related to the steel. Eliminating multiple types of steel eliminated the potential for using the wrong steel at the wrong time or place.

Things were less expensive, transactions were simplified, and our outside processors functioned more smoothly.

In another case—we were able to switch several of the Quad 1 products over to a more common resin. Historically the resin had been split about 50/50 between two different resin types. While it took some work to convince the customers that the newer resin was actually preferable, we were again able to simplify the purchasing process, get more uniformity through the plant and ease the production flow. This simplification of raw materials let us set up resin storage silos on a Kanban basis. Managing the raw material flow of resin became a simple visual decision. If a storage silo was empty then the order was placed to refill it.

Whether it is packaging, resin, steel, coffee or hospital services— often if you take similar processes and figure out how to consolidate your raw material flow you can have a tremendous impact on simplifying the business.

Sometimes something as simple as always using the same size nut and bolt can be helpful. Often the final selection of some of these items is left up to the engineering department. Given the myriad of critical projects they need to work on—this can be totally off their radar screen.

QUESTIONS

- Do you have similar products that use different raw materials?

- Who decides what raw material is used in the company?

- Have you ever made an effort to streamline raw material as a specific objective?

- Are there additives, material choices, or other changes you can make to consolidate material.

CHECKLIST

- Sort your raw material by Quad 1 looking for the key raw materials.

- Look for any outliers that are causing noise.

- Review why you need different material from your Quad 1 and eliminate these.

- How do different raw materials impact your material handling of items within your company?

CHAPTER 11
VENDOR COLLABORATION

Vendor Education

DESCRIPTION

This tool involves an effort to work with your vendors and train them in terms of what you are trying to do with a pull through system. Vendors need to actually be trained in the process. Good vendor ranking systems can go a long way to educating vendors—but it can also be a tedious and non-value added part of the process. The risk is that it becomes more about passing an exam and less about learning. Helping vendors understand the benefit of participating in a pull through process can be challenging. But once on board it can become a self-sustaining system. The most important part of this is that you need to make certain that you pay your vendors on time. They will be much more responsive this way.

You also want to focus on making the receipt of products easy for you. You want to make certain that items are being received in your Kanban Quantities, packaging is simple and easy to work with, and that your required information is provided by your vendor.

APPLICABLE QUADS

This technique is critical across all of the Quads.

RELATED TOOLS

This tool works best with

Vendor Consolidation

Rolling Purchase Order System (RPOS)

Kanban—Inventory Management Systems

BENEFITS

The seamless working of the company and having your vendors feel like they are a part of the solution. You will also need them when you are doing your expense review as you figure out how to take expenses out of the product.

EXAMPLES

It usual takes time to train your vendors, but it is a critical investment. They need to understand many of the same concepts you are implementing within your organization; Kanban inventory management, Visual Management, and the importance of accurate information management. The most important part of this is the vendor reduction program so that you have a reasonable number of vendors.

In one case, we had to actually go to a vendor's location and help them set-up their own internal Kanbans since they continued to try to plan production rather than just using a simple, visual trigger system. In one operation, we found that the Engineering Department was populating the vendor list when new products were being manufactured. The Purchasing department would have to then go through and depopulate this list which meant that if Purchasing felt a vendor was more appropriate than the one chosen by Engineering department, Engineering would have to get Purchasing's approval. Since most of the projects were already late by the time the purchasing department received it, the purchasing department wouldn't have time to appropriately price items. Since each engineer had their own preferred vendor list, it turned out that there was a proliferation of vendors.

It wasn't until the vendor reduction program was put in place and the purchasing and engineering department started to work together that there was any traction established on trying to bring more order to the process.

QUESTIONS

- Have you done an 80/20 review of your vendors?

- Has someone in purchasing visited your key vendors?

- Have you checked to make certain vendors understand your new system?

- Has any vendor shut down your line because of the inability to deliver product?

- Who in your organization selects vendors?

CHECKLIST

- Do you have a checklist for your vendors?

- Do your vendors understand Kanban and your requirements?

- Have you made a list of critical aspects that are important to communicate with your vendors?

Vendor Consolidation

DESCRIPTION

You can only achieve true vendor consolidation after you have done your line simplification process for both the product you are selling and then the consolidation of your raw material.

This is a crucial part of simplifying your company. Most companies have several hundred vendors all supplying different parts. The vendor consolidation program has large implications to this system working. The value of properly managing your supply chain can't be underestimated. The ability to strip out work and processes can be tremendous if you have your vendors engaged.

Most business can get their strategic vendors down to 30-40% of their original numeric value after doing an 80/20 sort of the vendors. For most businesses under $100 million that we have worked with over the last ten years, this has been in the range of 40 to 50 critical vendors. Often they have about 300 to 400 vendors. Fifteen to twenty vendors typically make up the bulk of a supply chain.

APPLICABLE QUADS

This process is used to manage all of your raw material coming into the company. Quad 1 is the cornerstone driver of raw material needs. This provides base requirements and then you strip out raw materials from there.

How can you possibly get down to this number? Often you pick a vendor like a fastening house or a distributor and have them carry a lot of the parts for you. In one case we actually turned over a lot of vendors to a distributor. You might pay a little more for the item, but this allows you to work around the situation when you are not a large customers and thus don't have a lot of clout.

You want these vendors on a Rolling Purchase Order System or have what they supply to you as a C class item.

You will also want to make certain that you are a large enough customer to have them take the program seriously. If you are not, they will not be willing to pay enough attention to the system.

The key is setting up your raw material to get pulled through your company via Kanban and Producing at Pull-through Production Rate.

RELATED TOOLS

This package works best with your Kanbans, Rolling Purchase Order System, and Vendor Training.

Kanban—Inventory Management Systems

Rolling Purchase Order System

Vendor Education

Produce at Pull-through Production Rate

BENEFITS

Vendor consolidation has a number of benefits. The primary benefit is that you only have a few numbers of vendors to train. It is almost impossible to work effectively with 300 vendors, but you could visit 30.

You can also communicate with 30. If you see a surge in the demand for a pending item then you can call 30 vendors. You can't call 300.

These vendors are trained to work within the 80/20 system. This is typically managed by the purchasing department with the General Manager sitting in as necessary for impression and commitment.

Also the in-bound logistics are much easier to manage with fewer vendors. If you are asking your vendor to supply parts to you within five business days, then you want to make certain there is sufficient volume/mix of parts to warrant this type of delivery.

EXAMPLES

In one company we were able to get down to about 30 vendors. It was simple to work with them. We got the system down so well that we didn't even have purchase orders any more.

We just had releases. The visual bins would come over to shipping and receiving and the shipping and receiving manager would pull out his reorder sheet and check mark the box that we needed the goods.

This sheet would then be faxed to the vendor who would confirm it and fax it back.

The goods would be received and the sheet would be attached to the bill of lading and go up to accounting for entry and payment. We never even had a purchase order. The goods were just received into the company.

This reorder sheet looked like the one below. It was simple:

Exhibit 26
Kanban Reorder Sheet

Key Vendor: FAX Number

Address Attn: Purchasing Manager

Ship To:

Part Number One

Part Number Two

Part Number Three

Confirmation _____

Order Date _____

Delivery Date _____

This form should actually be attached to each Kanban of raw material or parts that come into the company. When the Kanban is empty, it is placed in a bin or shelf on the production floor and then reordered.

If your parts are small or are in bins, then you can actually include information like part number, vendor and quantity on a label attached to the bin. In this case, the bin becomes the reorder item – when it is empty, it is moved over to a reorder area and is marked or identified as being reorder.

You can also have a wall of parts where the vendors just come in and fill the bins. This is usually done on small, inexpensive parts that are standard in their composition and can just be placed in an area. This is typically referred to as vendor managed inventory (VMI).

QUESTIONS

- What is the 80/20 breakdown of your vendors?

- Do you have more than 50 vendors?

- Do you have several vendors for the same category?

- Fasteners and Packaging—how many vendors do you have?

CHECKLIST

- Have you sorted your vendors from highest to lowest?

- Have you done your 80/20 cut?

- Have you picked a master vendor for all odd items that are one-offs?

Rolling Purchase Order System (RPOS)

DESCRIPTION

The Rolling Purchase Order System is an excellent technique to simplify and eliminate transactions. It is an effective way to reduce inventory and simultaneously simplify the transactions and workflow of purchasing.

Set up an agreement that each vendor signs:

- They are required to carry at least 2-3 Kanbans of material on their plant floor.

- Kanban deliveries are made in one week from receipt of a release.

- They are expected to respond within 8 hours of a request to deliver product.

- The vendors manage their inventory and production cycle to ensure that you - their customer – always has product when you need it. As soon as a vendor starts to explain to you their production process, it is time to educate them or find a new vendor.

- Vendors need to maintain prices so that you don't constantly have to change or adjust purchase orders. Typically you are looking for a 60-90 day notice on any price change.

- You continually renew an agreement to purchase product from them. You agree to purchase up to 90 days supply of the product from them on their floor going forward so that they know they will not become stuck with the product.

- Sometimes you agree to purchase more than 3 months if the part itself requires that it be purchased in larger quantities. You work hard to avoid this.

- You pay these vendors on time. This is critical since you are already asking them to hold the inventory over time.

- Vendors are expected to bill you on a weekly basis. This minimizes the number of accounting transactions that occur in a company.

- It is the obligation of the vendor to maintain a steady flow of parts/SKU's into their facility so that they can continue to make more units and meet your demand.

- Kanban Quantities are set and reviewed once or twice a year. Releases can be made through purchasing, plant floor and/or shipping and receiving. Shipping and receiving is generally best with some type of trigger coming out of the production/service area.

The hardest thing about this is getting the entire system up and running, but once it is then you can push forward into other areas of your company. How does it work?

- Trigger from production tells shipping and receiving person to purchase product.

- Shipping and Receiving Person/Cell Lead/Purchasing Agent sends over release form to bring in additional product.

- Release form becomes the purchase order.

- Goods are received against the release form and signed for by the shipping and receiving department.

- Release Form, Bill of Lading, and Packing List are attached together to create receipt of goods.

- Items requiring inventory maintenance are entered via the Accounting Department as a Purchase Order and Closed out Immediately.

- Items not requiring inventory maintenance are matched up with the invoice and paid.

You want to try to expense as much as possible within the company. This allows the flow through the organization to be continuous.

Exhibit 27
Rolling Purchase Agreement

This agreement between the Vendor and the Customer addresses the purchasing responsibility of the customer and stocking responsibility of the vendor.

INVENTORY REQUIREMENTS

- Vendor Agrees to hold at least 2 Kanbans of inventory on their floor at all times for immediate shipment to Customer.
- Orders will be acknowledged within 24 hours of receipt.
- Order will ship within 5 working days from receipt of the order.
- Orders will be labeled and shipped according to customer's specifications.
- Customer agrees to purchase up to 90 days of stock from the vendor.
- Products and Quantities are listed on Schedule A.

PRICING ISSUES

- Vendor agrees to maintain pricing and will provide a 90-day notice on any price increases.
- However, if a price increase does occur, all current inventory will be sold at the old price.
- Payment Terms will be simple and consistent.

CANCELATION

- Agreement has a 90-day cancelation time frame.
- Vendor will be responsible for providing 90 days worth of product from the date of the cancelation notice.
- Payment Terms will remain the same.
- Upon cancelation by customer, vendor will immediately stop production of all units and coordinate their completion with customer. Vendor will immediately provide full count of product quantities.

Customer Approval:	Vendor Approval
Name _____	Name _____
Title _____	Title _____
Signature _____	Signature _____
Date _____	Go Live Date _____

APPLICABLE QUADS

This should be done with everything in your company. You will find that your Quad 1 items are the natural drivers for your larger purchases. It is your Quad 2 and Quad 4 items that drive many of the smaller, one-off purchases for your remaining multitude of vendors.

RELATED TOOLS

This goes in conjunction with your vendor consolidation program, line simplification process and visual, Kanban Inventory management. Going down to a core quantity of vendors is critical. Since if you are a larger customer to these folks then you will able to better extract demands and vendors will be unwilling to lose the business. They are definitely not going to short ship you 100 screws at four cents each when you are doing $200,000 a year with them.

Vendor Consolidation

Kanban—Inventory Management Systems

C Class Inventory Management

BENEFITS

The beauty in the system is that it simplifies transactions. The process of reordering things that you purchase day in and day out becomes automatic. It no longer needs to be managed by purchasing folks. When you take 95% of all the purchases in the company and set them up this way you eliminate all of the purchasing work.

This allows your purchasing people to focus on driving down prices. You are only committed with vendors for 90 days. Usually we have found companies to have blanket purchase orders extending well beyond 90 days. The commitment is pretty much a non-issue.

The problem with most small frequent deliveries in order to decrease your inventory is that it also increases the number of transactions that you have. It is the transactions and the processing that makes this approach unmanageable. The RPOS system eliminates a lot of the transactional noise.

When you are receiving weekly shipments on your core RM inventory then your turns become exceptional.

EXAMPLES

In one organization, we were able to go from 200 vendors down to about 40 vendors. The key vendors were able to be set-up on a Rolling Purchase Order System. We were able to set it up so that each vendor had its own sheet of paper. The Kanban bin or inventory reorder trigger would come up and the shipping and receiving person would then check mark the box and fax it. The vendors would then fax the confirmation back to us.

If there were issues or a line was shut down then the information would come up to the general manager's office.

We were able to manage the purchase of up to $5 Million worth of inventory this way. It was a remarkably simple system. This is the most effective method we have ever seen to manage the inventory of a business. However, it is difficult and somewhat tedious to set-up.

QUESTIONS

- Do you have vendors that you purchase from on a consistent basis?

- Are your vendors local and are they willing to carry stock?

- When you do your vendor sort – how many do you find make up your 80/20?

- Are your parts/service that you purchase consistent?

- Are there ways to consolidate your purchases?

CHECKLIST

- Have you been through your vendors and worked to consolidate them?

- Are you willing to work with your top vendors and get them set up?

- Are your parts consistent?

Simplifying the Management of Overseas Vendors

DESCRIPTION

The management of inventory from overseas vendors is probably the most problematic from a continual flow point of view.

If you are fortunate enough to have enough volume to warrant a steady flow of products then the best way we have found is to break demand into steady, predictable orders. You have your set safety stock of inventory – but you manage your order stream three months out. Three months out provides your vendors time to adjust while also providing you with a continual flow of product to meet your needs.

Say you need to bring in load goods in which you use 600 every six months – you would place your orders. You would order 100 every single month, placing orders in the following pattern:

Month 1	Month 2	Month 3	Month 4	Month 5	Month 6
100	100	100	100	100	100

If you need to adjust the quantity going out because your needs have changed, don't adjust the very next month – go out three. The strategy is to avoid going up and down every single month trying to micro manage your demand. The key is to have sufficient inventory in the beginning to avoid having the need to constantly adjust. If you have sufficient buffer stock inventory then you can keep the flow steady. Allowing the three-month lead time to account for variability in the demand making one addition or subtraction to adjust. Obviously if you have a long term trend line towards a change in your ordering pattern then you would adjust accordingly

APPLICABLE QUADS

Principally Quad 1. You need volume to make this work.

RELATED TOOLS

Vendor Consolidation

BENEFITS

Produces predictability in ordering patterns. This allows your vendor some sense of continual demand so that you can negotiate a better price. Also it allows the system to manage itself on a short-term timeframe. You don't need to consistently micro-manage it.

Since you can't expect to receive immediate shipments as you can with domestic suppliers, a consistent cadence is the next best way to manage the randomness that characterizes every business.

EXAMPLES

At one business we were able to go from over 300 vendors down to 70 vendors. This made the set-up and training of vendors much easier. If we anticipated a spike in demand then we would call the vendors and have them increase their number of Kanbans.

We had a consistent demand for product from a sister company overseas. The company had monthly forecast meetings trying to predict demand and then place orders based on these forecasts. On the surface it made intuitive sense, but the forecasts were often wrong which resulted in operations and purchasing scrambling to make product. A lot of the components came from overseas so there were a tremendous amount of airfreight shipments to cover wrong orders as well as excess inventory from things that weren't needed.

A statistical analysis revealed that 80% of the business had a steady, predictable flow and this amounted to only 22 SKU's. This section of the business was separated and orders for these 22 SKU's were pulled through using this process rather than trying to micro-manage to a monthly forecast that consistently changed. The remaining inventory for the 20% items was much easier to manage and when they did need to airfreight something out it was inconsequential.

QUESTIONS

- Do I have sufficient volume to set up a continual order cadence from an overseas vendor?

- Is there any one vendor that can operate for me as a consolidator of product?

- What is the delivery lead time from each overseas vendor?

CHECKLIST

- Have you done your 80/20 vendor sort?

- Have you determined safety stock such that you will not be constantly adjusting inventory?

- Have you communicated the new system and expectations to your vendors?

Produce at Pull-through production rate

DESCRIPTION

A pull manufacturing process is the ideal way to set-up a company. It is a simple cycle of; sell a product, make a product; sell a product, make a product. You only manufacture what you sell and the rest you allow to remain on your floor. Your inventory is capped by your Kanban quantities and systems.

APPLICABLE QUADS

This process applies to all of your Quads except for possibly some minor run product in Quad 2 and Quad 4. You may find there is some product where the volume is so low that you might run it every six months on some type of planned production. However, your Quad 1 products you want to have pulled through your manufacturing or service process.

RELATED TOOLS

This system works best when you have effectively set up your Kanban Systems (inventory management system) to create a continual flow of product. Also having a visual system in place to know when you are in trouble helps a lot. Rolling Purchase Order System helps pull the inventory through while the decentralized cell leads assist to manage the system. You will have a steady flow of inventory and be better able to staff and balance your lines.

Kanban—Inventory Management Systems

Rolling Purchase Order System

Decentralized Leads

BENEFITS

Using the Pull-through production rate System means you are meeting the needs of your customers. You are producing only what you sell. This allows you to assign cell leadership roles and then apply continuous improvement techniques to successfully manage and improve your cells.

Even more importantly it allows you to get into a steady cadence on your plant floor. This mitigates the Ferry Effect discussed previously since it allows a production process that makes what you need, not items that have parts that are available or according to a forecast from sales.

If your finished goods inventory is sufficiently high and the ordering patterns of your customers are not too chunky, you can get to a point where the plant tends to run itself.

Setting the proper finished goods Kanban is critical to the effective use of Pull-through production rate. Your kanban inventory operates as a buffer between the variability of your customers' demand and operating issues within your plant.

Your finished goods Kanban allows you time to prioritize the production flow through your company. If you are always breaking into your production runs to meet a customer's needs, then you must review your Kanban Quantities.

One of the benefits of a pull through system is that it allows you to create a self-enclosed loop. After you have established your Kanban system, you need to have some type of trigger within the company that creates a Kanban production order to fill your finished goods target.

TRIGGERS FOR PULL-THROUGH PRODUCTION RATE VISUAL PRODUCTION

The ideal trigger is visual:

- Empty Kanban bins or Kanban area.

- Typically a lot of systems used a card system so after the finished goods have been pulled then you would bring the card back to the production board.

- You can also use inventory levels on a computer system to trigger a production run. This works when you have solid inventory control and finished goods that are not within line of sight.

EXAMPLES

In one system—with multiple levels of production issues, machining, welding, painting, assembly and final shipment—we used a card system that would flow with the product all the way through the production cycle, but once the product was assembled—the cards would actually sit until the group of products were received back and sold.

This was especially useful because the product would actually go out of the company for painting, but by having a visual card system on the wall of what was out for painting you could quickly get a feel for what was out and when it was coming back.

Another system we have seen used is where you track the inventory and when the inventory gets down past a Kanban trigger point—you would then generate a production ticket. These production tickets go out to the plant floor and create a production order that goes to your production board. This production board is then used to manage inventory.

Why is a Kanban, pull through system ideal? Forecasting customer demand is exceptionally difficult and except for seasonality maybe beyond your ability to control—the old random walk theory. However, improving your ability to react to changing demands is what you want to focus on not trying to predict demand. Through proper inventory management and systems set-up you can achieve two critical items:

- Shorten the lead time from when you receive an aberrant order to when you can actually manufacture it.

- You can isolate within the system those items that have a steady cadence and those items that don't. If you have systems in place to manage those items which have a steady cadence then your ability to focus on those that don't goes up tremendously.

Using a planner or forecaster to plan production is inherently difficult. The level of difficulty goes up exponentially every time you add a task or a job.

A central forecast system is analogous to the communist system where you have someone trying to make a plan to meet a customer's needs based on a customer's historical purchasing. Given that you have lead time issues and processing issues – trying to create product on the other side to meet this demand is difficult.

When you make too much there is a high cost to the process since the product will tend to sit there. This is expensive. When you make too little – then you will back order customers and have operational interruptions. This is expensive. To accommodate the variability of orders the forecaster will typically make too much inventory. When you need to adjust you must constantly circle back to the beginning of your pipeline and adjust your inbound inventory.

One of the key mistakes that people make is that it is almost impossible to dial back unwanted raw material and WIP that is going through the system. If your forecaster is wrong and you order the wrong SKU's then you are going to have to receive it and use it. But if you are producing at the market demand rate, then your manufacturing needs are pulled through the company by orders rather than pushed through the company by planners.

With a forecast system, people often have a ramp up strategy for new orders they didn't plan, but what they don't have is a ramp down strategy for things they don't need. There is no automatic shut off to the system in most companies.

Another problem is that if people work to stay busy they continue to make more product – often it isn't the product you need, however, it is the one with the most available parts. This can often use up components and resources (like warehouse space) that you need when you go back into production of the other product.

Pull-through systems eliminate this.

In a Kanban, pull through system – the process is like a train – where everything gets pulled forward only when you sell a product – you will never over produce beyond what is already set-up in your Kanban system. However, there is a tremendous amount of work involved in initially setup the appropriate inventory levels and the systems. The system has a self-imposed check mechanism that shuts down production and inventory when it is set-up properly. The pull through system is like capitalism – you make your product when you sell your product. The market dictates what is made. There is no master planner in the company determining what gets made.

This system can be challenging to run if you have high variability of demand. Quantitatively, if you have a high standard deviation of orders (approximately 1.5)—then you might have problems with a Kanban system. However, you need to take a serious look at what is actually causing the variability.

Sometimes it is the internal policies of the company (i.e. freight) which is causing this, production issues that created a lot of back orders so that the orders all come out at the same time, or the inability of someone in customer service to manage the orders so that they come out to shipping in a steady way. There should be a random nature to the ordering pattern unless you have true seasonality.

Seasonality can be addressed by increasing your Kanbans of finished goods or just getting very good at managing the product flow through and finding any area where you can decrease stock levels. The first time you set-up your Kanban system you want to be generous with the Finished Goods Quantities until the system is in place so that you can flush out any teething issues and then worry about maximizing your inventory levels.

You can also work with your vendors to manage stock levels when you approach an up-coming seasonality issue – then you can call your vendors and ask them to get three kanbans on their floor rather than two kanbans. If you have done the proper vendor consolidation, this shouldn't be a problem.

QUESTIONS

- Variability of Demand—what does your ordering pattern look like for your Quad 1 products, and your Quad 2 and 4 products?

- What steps have you taken to smooth over the ordering pattern?

- Do you have any monuments in production process?

- What steps can you take to break these monuments down?

- What type of visual inventory triggers are you using to manage production?

- Is your finished goods inventory within line of sight of your production area?

CHECKLIST

- Have you determined what amount of Finished Goods would you need on your floor to manage your customers demands for two weeks at a time?

- Have you back flushed this inventory back over your customers' demands to see how many stock-outs if any you would have?

- Have you set up a visual, pull through system in your plant?

- Is it possible to set-up your facility with a visual system?

CHAPTER 12
COMPANY WIDE SIMPLIFICATION

Outsourcing

DESCRIPTION

Outsourcing can be a powerful tool. It occurs when you take processes or products that you are not especially good at manufacturing or servicing and have someone else make them for you.

APPLICABLE QUADS

This technique tends to focus on your Quad 2 and Quad 4 products.

RELATED TOOLS

Visual Systems

Consolidation Of Raw Material

Vendor Consolidation

BENEFITS

Having other people make or manufacture a product line can help you focus your business around your core products. In fact, you are already outsourcing anything you don't manufacture from scratch. Hospitals may provide diagnostic tests, but they might well outsource laundering sheets. The key here is to stay focused on those products and processes where you add the most value. Which processes can be hard to define but most often the owner or manager knows what process in the company is a core competency and which one is not.

Apple is a great company that outsourced the manufacturing of products, but kept control of the design and functionality. They knew their greatest strength and decided to focus on that side of the business.

While you are probably not going to outsource the items in your Quad 1 you might outsource certain processes. Outsourcing can be a great tool for dealing with your Quad 2 products. Again, this may involve outsourcing an entire product or process. Tasks or processes that need to happen offline tend to be ideal for outsourcing. This is especially true for things that require that you have large quantities of inventory coming into the company.

In several cases, we were able to set it up so that that the outsourcing company would carry the bulk of the inventory and feed it into us on a small continual basis.

Initially, you do your 80/20 sort and your quad analysis and decide what you definitely want to continue making. After this, you will likely discover a list of Quad 2 products that you still need to provide.

When this is the case, you look to outsource the manufacturing of the product. You want to seek out companies that can provide you with the products, but are not key competitors or folks that you could accidentally put into your space. You definitely don't want to set-up 20/80 competitors and provide them with the wherewithal to grow into 80/20 competitors. There are many small companies where your 20/80 is their 80/20. They will be very receptive and responsive to your needs.

You only want to use the outsourcing tool after you have done your product line simplification process.

EXAMPLES

A successful example of an outsourcing process was the converting of the rolls from 48" to 24" for cutting to make a specific product. The company was doing it internally, but would have to purchase large containers of the rolls in order to get a competitive price.

We found a local company that would purchase the 48" rolls, cut them to size and then hold them for us rather than our having to purchase large quantities. Since this new vendor already had a relationship with the original vendor they weren't required to purchase as much to meet minimum order quantities. They also had the tools and equipment to execute the cutting process better than the original company.

Only after we looked at the Quad 2 product and what made it complicated for the company did we start to explore solutions. However, the large inventory of rolls and complaints from the management about the 90-day lead time for raw material helped us focus on this particular issue.

This solution freed up warehouse space, working capital and simplified the process since the new vendor would purchase the bulk rolls and deal with the long lead times while we just issued releases against the order.

The roll slitting was way outside the core strength of the company. Their core strength was the laminating of the foam product. But the rolls had just always been cut internally.

QUESTIONS

- Are parts of manufacturing process time consuming or complex but not core to your business?

- Are there parts/processes that exist in your business that are dedicated to just Quad 2 or Quad 4 offerings?

- After you have in-lined your Quad 1 products are there still some processes that require you to do them in batch rather than one at a time.

- Are there parts of your business that require you to have specialized personnel within the company. Is this process a part of your core competency?

CHECKLIST

- Have you listed out the process/products that are problematic for you to manage?

- Have you challenged yourself as to why you sell the products and/or why you are involved in the process?

- Are there vendors who could assist with this process who are not competitors?

Sales, Marketing And Price

DESCRIPTION

Pricing your product properly is one of your most valuable tools in order to drive your customers to the proper decision. It is important that your Quads reflect the transactional costs and values that are brought into the market. The Quad process gives you the opportunity to look at your pricing approach and the gross margin being earned by different sections of your business.

APPLICABLE QUADS

Quad 1 customers tend to drive your business and typically have the smallest cost per transaction because the organization should be geared around manufacturing/providing products to them. By definition, they are your largest customers consuming the greatest quantity. You would expect that the Quad 1 customers would have the lowest gross margin. They have the most buying power and thus may drive the hardest bargain.

Quad 2 products, while staying competitive, should have a higher gross margin than the Quad 1 products since these are supplemental items you keep within your product offer in order to support your main customers. Typically they aren't as critical to your customers either so you should be able to make a little more. You just don't want to be too aggressive and provide your competitors with a way into your customer base. It is not just about providing the product, but also about doing so at a competitive price.

Quad 3 customers' gross margin percentage should be higher than Quad 1 since they are purchasing in smaller, possibly more frequent, orders. There should be a higher transaction cost associated with these folks since smaller customers tend to cause more noise. These customers benefit from the Quad 1 customers that sustain your business.

The lack of pricing discipline within many organizations and the amount of money given way especially down in Quad 3 can be striking. We prefer to see at least a 10% greater gross margin in Quad 3 than Quad 1.

Quad 4 pricing should be the highest selling price and gross margin. If you are going to have the complexity and the smaller orders then you want to have these customers properly reflect their cost to the company. This should be significantly higher. These are the littlest guys. They need to be released or transferred or you need to decide to target them as items benefiting from attention and investment. Often these customers help drive product innovation and development efforts—customers who represent entry points into larger markets. Typically, we like to see Quad 4 products priced 15-20% higher than Quad 1.

RELATED TOOLS

The price component works well with line simplification. You can drive your customers to the right decision by making strategic pricing decisions towards your core products.

Product line simplification

BENEFITS

The obvious benefit is that you can improve your bottom line significantly. Solid pricing discipline in an organization can simplify order entry mistakes and make life easier across the entire transactional process.

You can also look at the Quad 3 customers and make certain you get the proper return. The Quad 3 customers should be paying more for the product than your Quad 1. If you decided to retain a Quad 4 product/customer then you also want to make certain that you are properly compensated for the complexity being introduced to the company.

EXAMPLES

In one transformation we were looking at the product mix in Quad 4 and it became apparent that there were number of universities and government researchers purchasing high tech variations of the product. They had a lot of special requirements, didn't pay a premium, and ended up using a lot of engineering time. It wasn't until we were going through the data that the enormity of this revealed itself. It came up as a key finding when one of the engineers involved in the process made the comment that a lot of the Quad 4 customers consumed the bulk of the engineering time.

When we investigated further the impact on the company, all of the manufacturing folks struggled getting these "specials" made. However, universities had access to the Engineering Department who actually loved the complexity and challenge of their product requirements. In some cases the engineers had developed a close relationship with university customers. A lot of the work being done in Engineering was being driven by these relationships.

On the surface, this sounded like leading edge development work and the kind of items you might want in your Quad 4.

However, when we dug down a little deeper the work wasn't and didn't appear like it would foster any real new product development or innovation for the Quad 1 customers. It wasn't developing any new impactful revenue streams or value creation. There were five engineers on staff and three of them spent most of their time focusing on custom making machinery for Universities and Researchers while only having a smattering of their team focused on their Quad 1 customers since these products were already up and running smoothly in the organization.

Furthermore, most of the products were in Quad 4 and had high gross margins. It appeared as if the Quad 4 products were highly desirable based on margin. The margins, however, didn't reflect the Engineering time, or the complexity that the products were bringing into the company.

These decisions should be made through a strategic process rather than just randomly occurring within an organization.

Whether you would want to continue this practice is up to the organization. In this case, the Universities who were requesting this special kind of assistance saw the price of their "Custom" units rise substantially.

QUESTIONS

- Does the Gross Margin Percentage in Each Quad Make Sense in relation to each other?

- Can you increase price in Quad 2, 3 or 4 without impacting your core business?

- What products are Quad 3 and 4 customers purchasing?

- Does your pricing reflect the transactional cost of doing business with each customer?

CHECKLIST

- Have you sorted you products/customers by contribution margin highest to lowest and looked for data points that seem inconsistent.

- Do you have a 10% larger gross margin in the Quad 3 than in Quad 1?

- Do you have a 20% large gross margin in the Quad 4 than in Quad 1?

- What is the percentage spread in amongst these Quads'?

- Are some customers carrying other customers within each Quad?

Transactional Analysis (Stapling Yourself To An Order)

DESCRIPTION

Another side aspect of this 80/20 review is the transaction analysis. Some folks refer to this as Order to Cash (OTC).

In this case, you want to take an order and walk your way all the way through the company, looking at the processes involved in taking an order all the way to cash. You are trying to simplify the process; removing unwanted steps.

Does information flow smoothly from department to department? Are there unnecessary steps whereby a shift in a procedure to a different department can streamline things? How much circular logic is there?

Where does the order enter the production planning process? Ideally it is at the end of the system as finished goods. However, if you are a made to order company this can be more difficult to manage.

This is a detailed analysis listing out all of the various decision points. The analysis involves laying out all of the steps involved in the OTC and then reviewing these steps one by one to search for opportunities to strip out redundancy. The problem with this process is that it typically isn't game changing. It is more modest simplification, rather than a true transformation of the business. However, it can be very effective at removing unneeded complexity. You can also improve your cash flow by shipping orders faster and turning inventory more frequently.

APPLICABLE QUADS

You look for your Quad 1 orders to be pretty streamlined without a lot of steps involved in the system.

RELATED TOOLS

This is something that can be completed in a standalone environment. It is a standard go-to technique for lean practitioners.

Product line simplification

Produce at Pull-through Production Rate

Kanban—Inventory Management Systems

BENEFITS

Simplifying the business and its processes.

EXAMPLES

In one recent company, there was a system where orders were placed on hold when they needed changes or customer specific information. These same orders ran through the credit department and every time the order changed the order would re-circulate through the credit department. There were times when an order was touched eight different times by these two departments without any thought as to the exact issue or need for these two departments to double check everything. It had simply always been done that way. In some cases, orders were being run through the accounting department when simple instructions were being changed such as shipping addresses rather than being taken care of in customer service.

The process was redesigned to assess whether an order was "credit worthy" when first received. Once accepted, order changes were the responsibility of customer service and orders were not re-circulated through accounting. We suspected that the original policy was put in place when a customer slipped through the system by changing an order. However, whatever value the prior policy added for the organization had disappeared and it now was just causing redundancy.

QUESTIONS

- Have you designed each step from customer service all the way through the receipt of the cash?

- How long does the transaction reside in each area and why?

- How many paths are there for the order to wander off track?

- How often does someone have to go outside of their group for an answer?

CHECKLIST

- Did you flow chart all of the orders?

- Did you walk the flow of the orders through the company?

- Did you question each person who participates in the process for thoughts on what would make it more productive?

Point Of Use

DESCRIPTION

Point-of-use is a simple concept. We all live it every single day of our lives; however, there are times when we don't effectively carry over parts of personal life into our business life.

Simple question—where do you keep your toothbrush? Unless you are really a special and interesting person, it is probably next to the sink where you brush your teeth. This is a simple example of point-of-use.

Some companies, however, keep key tools and equipment separate from where the process actually occurs. They either move tools and equipment towards the product or move product towards the tools and equipment.

Usually this is done because the number of tools required for a production area changes depending upon the product being run. This is where the line simplification comes in as you figure out how to rearrange your equipment needed to support a trimmed down product offering and dedicate equipment to your production process for Quad 1 products. Equipment ought to be close to its point of use. Sometimes you have to think differently about the production process to accomplish this.

People are point of use. One of the key concepts that people miss about point-of-use is that the concept applies to personnel as well. Your warehouse foreman should be in the warehouse, preferably with his desk in the warehouse shipping and receiving area. This is their domain and this person should know every single item that comes and goes out the plant.

Production planning and management staff should be based in the plant; preferably with a desk on the plant floor. That way, they are not hiding in an office away from their people looking at some computer screen. You want to make certain that the information people need to run their area is visible and available to everyone. **Information is point of use.**

You want to make certain that the information they need in order to run their business is visible to everyone and they can respond to issues in the plant as needed. The point-of-use people can be likened to referees on a football field—they need to be making calls in the middle of the game, rather than in some back room.

The Lean Techniques taught in the Toyota Production System is a great list of general wastes involved in an organization. These seven wastes within an organization are listed below.

1.   Waste of over production.

2.   Waste of time on hand (waiting).

3.   Waste of transportation.

4.   Waste of processing itself.

5.   Waste of stock at hand.

6.   Waste of movement.

7.   Waste of making defective products.

Point of Use helps eliminate the core issues of the waste of movement, the waste of transportation, and the waste of time on hand.

APPLICABLE QUADS

Point of Use is particularly applicable to Quad 1 items. Make certain that the tools, inventory, and personnel are always there, including what you need to make any type of change over in the line.

RELATED TOOLS

Point of Use along with Dedicated Equipment, Kanban and Cell Balancing and Cell Management all work in unison to make for an effectively managed cell. These are the tools cell leads need to be truly effective in their job.

Dedicated Equipment

Decentralized Cell Leads: Autonomy, Ownership and Empowerment

Kanban—Inventory Management Systems

In-Lining Operation

BENEFITS

Point of use is effective because it eliminates a lot of wasted time looking for an item. It makes a visual system more effective because it places the user within close visual proximity to the product.

Obviously, the benefit of eliminating walking and/or down time is helpful. However, the stronger, more beneficial aspect of this technique is accountability and control. This places the equipment and the inventory in the area of the person using. Because the items are in the domain of your cell leader it is much easier to hold them accountable for making certain they have the proper inventory or that the equipment is functioning.

This is often a huge cultural shift for an organization. What you are doing is transferring ownership and responsibility onto the plant floor. If you set-it up correctly the cell manager can no longer blame someone in purchasing for not getting the right part or getting that correct part in time. It becomes their responsibility during the daily Gemba walks to make certain they have what they need to run production. It eliminates a tremendous amount of finger pointing and the feeling that management is in control and the product floor work is just supposed to do what they are told. Now your floor workers are a part of the team managing production. This drives productivity.

EXAMPLES

One company that we recently transformed had over 200 SKU's in their finished goods offerings. Two production planners worked with the forecast to predict what they would need to manufacture each month. These two planners routinely scanned reports trying to properly manage and predict inventory needs. Exhibit 28 is a photograph of the production board the company used to support this process. The lower portion of the board lists the parts needed to manufacture product that were out of stock. Production for the week was completely shut down.

Exhibit 28
Original Production Board

The company had no finished goods and the production meetings were really about what we could make that day based on parts availability.

Critical steps taken to fix the problem:

- Transformed the production meeting into a Gemba Walk.
- Set-up and established a visual Kanban System.

- Pushed the pending production out onto the plant floor so it was visible to the line leads.

- Established a Finished Goods Kanban as a buffer.

- Empowered the line leads to be accountable for keeping their lines running.

This all took about six months to establish. The efficiency and productivity of the facility increased dramatically because the company now had the parts they needed in order to make their product. The new visual production board is shown in Exhibit 29.

Exhibit 29
Redesigned Visual Production Board

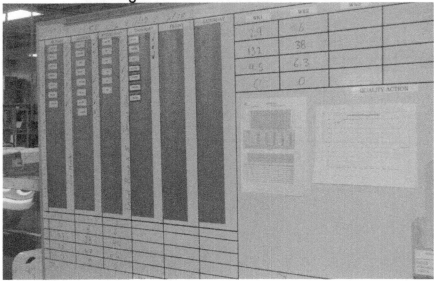

If you look at the redesigned production board, you will see that all parts are in stock and production was running on a steady, daily basis. Why is this an example of point of use? It is about the ownership and cell management and having the tools and information out in the area where it is used. In this case, we took the management decision making process and made it point of use (Gemba Walk). We posted information not only on the inventory issues but also pending production and made it point of use. Through a visual Kanban System, cell leaders were now in charge of the inventory they needed to get their work completed. This control was made point of use.

Via the cell leadership tool we empowered cell leaders to use the information and make decisions within their work area to better manage and run their areas. This had the additional benefit of more fully engaging the production staff in the smooth operation of the line.

QUESTIONS

- When you see people walking outside of their work area – do you often stop and ask them why?

- Are your operational employees stationed in their work area or are the offices comfortably tucked in with other management people?

- How many material handlers do you have in the company?

- Do your employees have the tools and information they need in order to do their job properly?

CHECKLIST

- Is your inventory in the cell/operational area?

- Are the tools and equipment available that are needed within each cell?

- Have you posted the key metrics needed to manage the cell?

- Do your Cell Leads have all the information they need to run each area?

Triad Business Structure

DESCRIPTION

The Triad Structure is a system we have seen work well in small to medium firms. The intent of the structure is to develop a set of clearly defined rules that promote a level of accountability within each department.

The interest is to have an organization where each department has the responsibility and accountability to run their area interacting with the other areas on a regular basis.

As the name suggests, three primary functions work together in the system:

1.   Operations

2.   Shipping and Receiving/Warehouse

3.   Customer Service/Sales

OPERATIONS

- Determines what is manufactured given certain needs from a visual, pull through production process. They are manufacturing to a Kanban level of finished goods.

- Works to streamline the manufacturing process – focused and dedicated.

- Responsible for receiving the raw material from the shipping and receiving area, inspecting the raw material and putting it back on the Kanban shelf.

- Moves empty Kanbans over to warehouse for Receiving.

- Insures quality of product.

- Notifies Shipping and Receiving of any parts that are running low.

- Works with Customer Service/Sales to coordinate any unusual orders or situations.

SHIPPING AND RECEIVING/WAREHOUSE

- Reorders all of the supplies for the entire company on a Kanban System.

- Manages the Finished Goods Warehouse.

- Receives raw material and makes certain that the goods are properly marked and ready for receipt by the Production Area.

- Ships all outgoing orders.

- Manages freight.

CUSTOMER SERVICE/SALES

- Receives and enters orders.

- Prints pick tickets and orders.

- Invoices orders to keep a record of what has shipped.

- Notifies production of any customer issues and reviews the production schedule to see when material is being made.

- Works with shipping and receiving to make certain all the orders went out and account for any situations where the order has to be expedited or the order is exceptionally large (added from point of use section).

- Works with the freight companies.

These three areas of responsibility form the basic triad. The three lists we included reveal that while there are distinct chains of command within each of the three areas, daily cooperative efforts between the areas is crucial to the success of a business.

Employees need to have a hand shake arrangement as they pass responsibility from one functional area to the other functional area.

APPLICABLE QUADS

This process applies to the management of the business as a whole.

RELATED TOOLS

This works best after you have simplified the business unit and simplified processes across the unit.

Line Simplification

BENEFITS

Creates clearly defined roles and accountability within the system. It also empowers the individuals within their system to focus and maintain their area.

EXAMPLES

Not applicable.

QUESTIONS

- Does each area within your company have the tools and resources needed to get their job done on a daily basis?

- If they don't have what they need is there a visual metric posted in organization so that you know when they are running low?
- Is each area of responsibility well defined and in the control of the person responsible?

CHECKLIST

- The raw materials needed to manufacture the product or provide the service are available to the operators making the product. In other words, the operators don't need to ask anyone to get stuff for them.
- Are the Kanbans/orders clearly posted for the operators/service providers so they know what is needed and when?
- Is there a system in place for them to know when they are running behind?
- Is there a daily meeting between the Floor, Shipping and Receiving and the Head Customer Service Manager?

Crossover Thresholds

DESCRIPTION

Crossover thresholds come from your red light/green light analysis and are the point where the product or customer goes from being 20/80 to 80/20.

APPLICABLE QUADS

This is primarily Quads 1 and Quad 4.

RELATED TOOLS

This would work with your line simplification process. It is a part of integrating the 80/20 process into your company.

Product Line Simplification

BENEFITS

You use the crossover threshold when you are going through your line simplification process to see how close a product and/or customer is to moving into Quad 1.

This tool is most effective as you work to include the Quad work as a part of your future budgeting process. Any project or customer that does not have sufficient projected gross margin above the crossover threshold needs a lot of review. It is a major red flag if new products or customers drop below this threshold.

EXAMPLES

Not Applicable

QUESTIONS

- How are new products and customers introduced into your business?

- What systems do you have in place to keep new complexity from entering the company?

- Who decides what new products to add?

- Are there products or customers that could move into Quad 1 by adding new products to their mix?

CHECKLIST

- Do you have crossover thresholds in your organization?

- Have your reviewed the process of adding new items to your offering?

PART 4
TURNING INSIGHTS INTO DELIVERED CHANGE

CHAPTER 13
EXECUTING AGAINST YOUR INSIGHTS

Organizations, like people, are creatures of habit. We design organizations to be controlled and predictable. Henry Ford, in the earliest days of the assembly line, lamented that workers kept insisting on thinking for themselves rather than simply executing their prescribed tasks mechanically. The analytical tools and techniques we have described are essential to identify where to focus your efforts and to identify what needs to be done. **Until we also know how to execute the change to move the organization from what it does today to what the organization needs to do tomorrow, our analytical insights will only identify hypothetical benefits.**

"New and better" will always be considered suspect compared to "tried and true." Regardless of how powerful the arguments and analyses pointing toward the new or better, the forces for stability always have the advantage. If there is to be any hope of adapting to a changing competitive environment or taking advantage of short-lived opportunities, this organizational bias for stability must be taken into account and counter-balanced if organizations wish to exploit the opportunities identified in our analysis.

To move an organization from insight to action requires you to address two challenges. First, understand the forces required to promote organizational stability (and increase the risk of organizational stagnation). Understand how these stabilizing forces surface and manifest as multiple forms of resistance to proposed changes. Second, develop the organizational capacity to design and manage multiple interacting projects. These tasks are equally challenging in most organizations because organizations are built around processes as well as organizational functions. Projects will often differ in critical ways from the familiar and comfortable status quo.

Throughout this effort we have emphasized the importance of thinking about and acting on the organization as an integrated system. Organizational silos that restrict the flow of information between functions and departments are a natural byproduct of carving the system into specialized components. Silos become a problem when the basis for setting organization boundaries becomes obsolete and good decisions demand communication and coordination across the boundaries of those silos.

The analytic tools and techniques we have discussed up to this point are grounded in two simple beliefs. One, an organization can always improve. Two, you can tune and balance the organization, or system, as a whole to improve it. You cannot optimize the individual parts and expect to do as well as you can when treat the organization as an integrated whole.

We also believe that the particular tools and techniques we recommend identify better improvement opportunities than other methods. Our 80/20 reviews and our Quad analyses set an agenda focused on the most consequential and high impact opportunities within the enterprise. Depending on the particular issue or opportunity, the other tools in our toolkit provide the specific techniques and guidance that allow us to tackle that opportunity. Transforming opportunities into realized benefits, however, is not simply a matter of identifying the opportunities and expecting that the organization will magically "make it so."

No analysis of an opportunity ever produced benefits. There are no free lunches. There is always a design and execution effort to translate potential into realized benefits. Even the simplest seeming change to stop selling a poor-performing product, for example, requires some effort to execute. Perhaps the product catalog needs to be updated or an email drafted to inform the sales force and current customers. Will we sell whatever inventory remains of the product before or after we announce the change?

Tackling any specific opportunity calls for a project and projects must be managed like any other activity. Taken as a whole, a systematic review will identify dozens of attractive ideas and potential initiatives. Each idea or initiative represents a possible project. Each possible project can divert attention from keeping the existing business running smoothly and call on resources that are in scarce supply. Each will disturb and disrupt the existing organization in ways that are both intended and unintended.

This is the realm of project and change management. Organizations that are adept at managing operations and sales are not necessarily similarly adept in the realm of projects and change. This relative lack of skill and experience gets labeled as "resistance to change." That is an overly broad and unhelpful characterization. We need to dig deeper to better understand how to translate hypothetical benefits into the kind of real transformation that MIP and others have achieved.

"Interesting, but it will never work here"

Wherever we have applied this approach and made the transition from insight to execution, we have realized a 10% or better improvement in profitability within a year. ITW has had similar results over the course of more than 800 acquisitions. However, the most frequent response we hear when first presenting this evidence is "interesting, but it will never work here."

The objections take multiple forms. "We're a job shop, every order is customized." "Our leads times from customers are too short." "Our bills of material are too complex." "Our products are commodities, we have to compete on customer service." All are variations of "our business is unique." Successful businesses are always on the quest to be unique in some way. That quest, however, actually has little direct bearing on the search for uniqueness, or differentiation. Our approach identifies improvements that eliminate complexity yet does not affect an organization's competitive uniqueness.

Second, these objections require sensitivity to the motivations and expectations of management, especially those who lead organizations in the neglected middle. Managers and executives work hard to make their organizations prosper and succeed. They are intimately familiar with their products, operations, and customers. No one is keen to hear that they have missed an opportunity that is apparent to outsiders with a spreadsheet. They are especially skeptical after they have already invested in Six Sigma training, experimented with applications of lean manufacturing, or invested in one of the individual tools and techniques we discussed earlier.

Those organizations that have made a sustained commitment to the evidence-based, systemic approach to continuous improvement that we advocate are more open to the possibility of learning something new. The organizations that have adopted and applied our methods are more successful than those who have dabbled with individual tools and techniques as they fall in and out of fashion.

The statement that "it will never work here" conceals an important dilemma about bridging the gap between analysis and execution; between knowing and doing. The conventional view of this gap is the well-deserved disdain experienced executives feel toward freshly minted MBAs or young consultants in expensive suits. Finding the "right" answer is only an early step in the path toward changing how an organization operates. The frustration of watching organizations cling to the comforts of "we've always done it this way" is the flip side of this gap.

This gap cannot be bridged with a better analysis or a more effective presentation. Use the analytical process together with the detailed knowledge of the existing organization and its history of the project team insiders to bridge the gap. The most effective way to build that bridge is understand that implementation and execution begin during the earliest stages of the analysis. The analysis cannot be outsourced. One of the principal benefits of the improvement in data availability and the power of analytical tools is that those who bring a deep understanding of their organization and its history can be more fully engaged in the analysis.

The challenge is to ensure that those with company knowledge and history are an integral part of the process from the outset. There is often a temptation to seek short-term efficiencies in the early stages of the analysis. That is usually a mistake. On the one hand, the analysis can drift without the experience and insight of the right insiders. Much more importantly, however, successful execution depends on the engagement and commitment of insiders with the power needed to generate and sustain the energy for change. This analytical process itself builds engagement and commitment.

Limits of Quad Mapping

Are there places where 80/20 analysis and the data driven approach doesn't work? Start-ups generally haven't yet reached a level of complexity where these tools have a major impact. When you are engaged in a start-up, your goal is to avoid adding complexity in the first place. Organizations with narrow product lines or narrow customers bases are also less likely to benefit from this approach.

Some organizations rely on highly customized approaches to customers. Every product and service is tailored. In those settings it may not be immediately evident how and where to apply 80/20 thinking. Even then, the discipline of 80/20 thinking and line simplification can direct a search for simplifications hiding behind unintentional complexities.

For example, we recently converted a company from a forecast production system to a finished goods model. The existing forecast system was messy and the plant was consistently shut down due to lack of parts. On time delivery was erratic with customers often waiting for delivery of the orders. The existing forecasting model predicted manufacturing needs with 65% accuracy. The assumption in the company was that the variability in customer demand was too high to justify any type of finished goods inventory strategy.

The 80/20 analysis of products, however, revealed that nearly 80% of sales came from only 23 SKUs. Remaining sales were one offs that had to be managed through longer lead times in the company. We carved out these 23 models to stock in finished goods inventory. Rather than build these to order, we manufactured them on a regular Kanban, Pull-through production rate system as explained in the toolkit. The remaining models were only manufactured as they were ordered. What we found was that this finished goods Kanban system was able to predict 80% of the companies manufacturing needs for the month versus the 65% accuracy of the previous forecast system. Differentiating between the core 23 models that covered 80% of demand and all the other models, made it possible to tune the production system. We worked with the company to develop a continual build, highly efficient system for the 23 models (and 80% of revenues) that we knew we would need each month. Improved efficiency and building to finished goods inventory made it possible to also improve the efficiency of producing the irregular and unpredictable orders constituting the rest of sales. The combination of production efficiencies and the consequent increase in available capacity reduced lead times for some build to order products from ten to three days improving their profitability as well.

This company had dismissed using some of the tools in the toolkit to simplify their business model because of the preconceived notion that their ordering pattern was too unpredictable. Through the data analysis, we were able to differentiate the predictable from the unpredictable and develop separate systems to manage what was predictable. The company had to move beyond the belief that "it will never work here" and see the implications of the analysis. The results were tremendous. On-time delivery shot through the roof and the end of the month seemed like any other day rather than being complete chaos. 80% of the SKU's were in stock ready to ship and then the remaining 20% were ushered through the organization without incident and much better focus.

Committing to Organizational Change

Two observations about change and resistance are relevant. First, organizations are designed to be stable. Manufacturing and production processes are designed and evaluated on their consistency and lack of variation. Organizational departments and functions are designed to insulate and isolate key elements of the organization from the external environment. This stability becomes a problem when the external environment is changing faster than the capacity of the organization to adapt. Change, particularly rapid and externally forced change, is not part of the average organization's repertoire.

The second observation is that resistance is more often a function of imposed change rather than simply change. People and organizations are much more likely to change if they view themselves as integrally involved in both the decision to change and in the change itself. As a simple example, consider the number of people switching to smartphones and sharing app recommendations within their circle of friends and coworkers.

ITW, for example, has one tremendous advantage over other organizations in implementing change. ITW is permeated with a shared belief and commitment to the analytical tools and techniques of 80/20 analysis, Quad mapping, and the systematic and integrated use of the toolkit. Managers are expected to commit to and follow the program. Those with reservations are invited to look for other employment opportunities. This commitment from the ITW organization as a whole has a powerful impact on the success rate of transformation. Failure is not an option.

Other organizations are more skeptical. The benefits are hypothetical while the costs of change appear intimidatingly high. Conventional wisdom holds that people and organizations fear and resist change. You can perform the best analysis possible, but if you can't successfully execute the necessary changes then your work has been for naught. Understanding the barriers and impediments to change must be understood and addressed if organizations want to realize the benefits of this process.

Reframing Resistance to Change

Effective change starts with learning. Those advocating change and those questioning it must both participate in the learning process. Blanket statements that "everyone fears change" aren't terribly helpful for this is not only a cliché, it's wrong. Certainly, many have anxieties about the unknown and prefer the stability of the known. At the same time, there are nearly as many who are excited and drawn to the new and different; they seek out change and can be stifled by routine. Studies of innovation have consistently found a predictable distribution of attitudes and approaches toward innovation. Most managers and executives have seen some form of the following graph:

Exhibit 30
Uptake in Innovations over Time

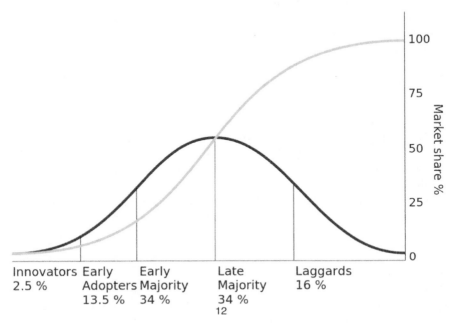

Marketing and product managers plan their product introductions and roll outs based on this predictability. They target "Innovators" and "Early Adopters" to drive product uptake. They tailor communication strategies to the predictable concerns and biases in each stage.

This same distribution of concerns and biases applies to innovation within organizations. Any large-scale change in processes or practices will encounter the full distribution of responses from Innovators to Laggards. Within organizations this is further complicated because the distribution of Innovators, Early Adopters, and the like is independent of the distribution of organizational power and authority. Project managers need to take both innovation attitudes and organizational power into account as they develop their project plans. Effective project managers ignore blanket assumptions that people "resist change." Their stakeholder analysis, for example, would consider how to take advantage of an Engineering Director who is predisposed to innovation to offset a powerful and skeptical CFO.

Organizations that reap the greatest benefit are those that build a bridge between "it will never work here, we are unique" and "it has worked everywhere else where it's been done seriously." This proves to be less about overcoming resistance and more about developing an effective learning partnership between those who see new possibilities and those with deep industry and organizational experience.

The concrete evidence developed during the 80/20 analysis and Quad mapping provides an objective basis for a productive dialog between those with a fresh perspective on the data and those immersed in the current environment. Rather than a futile "new way good, old way bad" dialog 80/20 analysis permits a conversation about "why does the data contradict our experience." Instead of an adversarial conversation, the evidence allows, at least potentially, for a joint exploration for insight.

Promoting dialogue between hard evidence and long experience shows that the earlier you involve someone with deep organizational experience in the process the more value you derive from the process. An example of a hidden problem that resisted analysis until we tapped the right organizational history surfaced during an 80/20 review with a major meatpacking company.

In a meatpacking company, livestock goes in and boxes of chops, ribs, and other cuts come out at the other end of the production process. A tour of operations will make most anyone at least a temporary vegetarian. On the other hand, nothing goes to waste; profitability depends as much on the price of bone meal as it does for prime cuts of meat. In an analysis of product sales, we were particularly concerned with the price of fat. Standard reports derived from the existing information systems showed the cost of fat as nine cents a pound. Our analyses, however, kept arriving at a value of twelve cents per pound. This discrepancy had the potential to have a significant, and possibly material, impact on the overall financial results for the organization, given the sheer number of pounds processed every day through the operation.

After several rounds of review, meetings with the CFO, and multiple recalculations we ultimately traced our way back to a programmer in the information systems group nearing retirement. As we were starting to explain our problem, the analyst interrupted us to explain that when the original system had been deployed there had been no way to calculate all the costs dynamically. The nine cents per pound price for fat had been set as a constant when the previous system had been deployed years earlier and never changed. What was a sensible decision at the time was now pushing managers in the direction of poor pricing decisions.

This is one example of the often hidden assumptions that may make current data questionable. Someone with deep organizational experience is needed, before an analysis can conclude, to discern whether the data represents a problem that needs to be fixed or provides a picture of the organization that can be trusted.

CHAPTER 14
MANAGING EXECUTION–LEARNING TO DO PROJECTS

To this point we have focused on an evidence-driven approach to identify opportunities for improvement and specific tools and improvement techniques for the various areas of opportunity. Knowing the right answer, however, is only a tiny piece of putting those insights into practice. We are now in the realm of how to make organizational change happen, a topic acknowledged as critical to success in theory and often botched, even ignored, in execution. There are many reasons for this paradox. We'll touch on them as we discuss our experience in getting execution to work.

Organizations are designed and built to reliably execute processes. McDonalds makes money for itself and returns for its shareholders providing products, service, and experience that is remarkably, reliably, and predictably similar wherever you encounter a McDonalds. They do this by carefully designing, testing, and controlling every detail of the products, facilities, processes, practices, pricing, promotion, and staffing. Organizations, McDonalds included, rarely devote the same level of obsessive attention when they plan and execute change projects.

Juggling competing projects

The first element of working systematically is to attack problems and opportunities in good order. Second tackle each problem and opportunity in a way that allows the organization to get better at the process of addressing problems over time. Build organizational muscle memory. Treating each problem/opportunity in an ad hoc way diminishes and dissipates the organization's capacity to learn and improve over time—to become better at the process of getting better.

An obstacle to organizational change is that project management skills are routinely undervalued. Fame, glory, and resources go to those who manage functions and processes—the elements of perceived stability and permanence in organizations. Project management skills are less valued and consequently less developed. The success or failure of the improvement opportunities identified through this process depends heavily on adequate project management skills and capacity.

Manage the analytical and execution work we have been discussing as discrete projects; each with a distinct beginning, middle, and end. These projects are mostly small to medium-scale efforts. Many are largely independent of one another. On the other hand, there will also be key dependencies among some of the project efforts. Likely, enough projects will be identified to require dedicated personnel to assess and manage the overall demands on the organization and its workforce.

For all of this project activity, few of us have significant training in project management or in how projects differ from our routine management responsibilities. In too many organizations, if you are assigned part time to four different projects (not unusual for someone in middle management), you will likely encounter four different approaches to run the projects and integrate your expertise. This is not a recipe for high levels of personal or organizational effectiveness. Nor is it a recipe for manageable levels of stress.

Today's project management world focuses on the extremes. On the one hand, there is a substantial knowledge base on the challenges of mega-projects such as the efforts to implement enterprise resource planning systems (ERP) such as Oracle and SAP. These projects typically demand significant outside expertise and sophisticated tools and techniques. The Project Management Institute certifies project management professionals. The organization recently released the third edition of the Project Management Book of Knowledge—which runs to several hundred pages. Project management professionals, like all experts, deal with complex and esoteric details to build their reputations. This level of scrutiny and detail is unnecessary for the kinds of projects we are talking about here. You are not likely, for example, to need a complex time-reporting system to track each individual's activities.

While the experts are pushing forward at the frontiers of complex project management, they have largely ignored the need to equip ordinary line managers to operate in the project-based world we now occupy. There is an absence of good support for the "projects in the middle" even though mid-sized projects are abundant in our environment. They are projects that must coordinate the efforts of a modest project team (anywhere from three to fifteen people) over a two to six month timeframe. This chapter focuses on mid-sized projects and on the additional challenge of coordinating multiple projects. This is a Swiss Army Knife approach to project management. Tools and knowledge enough to handle the routine challenges you will encounter plus guidance on times you might want something bigger than a pocket knife.

Project Management

Executing an 80/20 Quad transformation relies heavily on effective project management. Projects present different demands than managing a function or business process on a day-to-day basis. The projects identified in a Quad transformation draw heavily on the cumulative knowledge and experience of those who manage and work within these processes and functions. This knowledge base offsets the relatively lower level of project management skills and brings the task into the realm of the possible.

For any project, the end is where to begin. At its simplest, a project is a set of steps and tasks that will take you from point A to point B. Until you describe what the end needs to look like, you have no basis to map the effort it will take to create it. Imagine what you need to deliver in reasonable detail and you can work backwards to the steps that will bring it into being.

Working out those steps can be done with two tools and three rules. This is possible in large part because the earlier efforts in Quad mapping, line simplification, and the toolkit define point B with a good deal of specificity. For each prospective project identified in the preceding analysis, these tools will yield a project plan that can be executed by the existing organization.

Tool #1: A messy outline. An outline captures the essential features of ordering steps and clustering them. Messy because you can't and won't get it right the first time and the neat outlines taught in middle school interfere with that. A messy outline encourages the necessary flexibility for creative problem solving.

Tool #2: A calendar. If you can do it all without looking at one, you aren't talking about a project.

Three rules will let you generate the substance of the outline:

Rule #1: Define small chunks of work.

Rule #2: Do first things first.

Rule #3: Group like things together.

If you can see how to get from A to B in a single step you don't have a project; instead you have an essential building block. "Small chunks" is a reminder that the only way to eat an elephant is in small bites. There are a variety of heuristics about recognizing what constitutes an appropriate small chunk of a project. Somewhere between a day and a week's worth of work for one person isn't a bad starting point.

Building a project plan starts with generating a list of small chunks of work. This list is the raw material that feeds a repetitive cycle to put first things first, group like things together, and revise the list of small chunks.

Small chunks of work may include:

- Schedule an interview with the inventory planner.

- Conduct the interview.

- Summarize your notes from the interview.

- Map the flow of raw materials from the receiving dock into inventory and out to a workstation on the production line.

- Shadow a sales rep on an initial sales call.

- Review a sample of recent sales orders and tabulating the information that is routinely missing.

- Prepare an 80/20 analysis of last quarter's sales by product SKU.

- Review the notes from interviews with 20 sales reps to identify common themes and recurring patterns.

Project managers get into trouble when they fail to identify relevant chunks of work. You will have a problem if you forget to put something into the plan that should have been there. When you do identify a missing task, at best you only have additional work to complete. If a forgotten task turns out to be a prerequisite for a subsequent task, forgetting it may bring an entire project effort and team to a standstill.

The overhead of running the project itself is a commonly overlooked task. Running a project calls for team meetings, status reports, reviewing the current plan, and handling staffing issues. While these tasks may not directly contribute to the final deliverable, you must still do them if you hope to complete the project in a finite amount of time.

It takes a mix of individual and group effort to generate a good list of tasks. Drawing on our individual experiences, we can each think of relevant and useful bits of work that will move us toward our destination. The team will identify more potential tasks and organize the entire list more intelligently when meetings around a whiteboard are held with all team members. For instance, if three team members want to interview the Director of Sales, a single interview will suffice. A fourth team member might point out that the team should also plan to interview the Sales Managers in each Region.

Sophisticated project management requires cleverness and insight when sequencing and clustering activities. For many projects, it is sufficient to focus on simply thinking through what needs to be done, the order to fulfill the tasks, before leaping to the first task. That's why an outline is a more useful planning tool than Gantt charts or Microsoft Project. An outline adds structure as compared with a simple to do list. An outline's simple structure prevents getting lost in the intricacies of a complex software tool. An outline helps you organize your work, helps you discover similar tasks, deliverables, or resources that can be grouped together in your plans. An outline allows you to order and cluster related tasks. For many projects this will be enough. For the rest, it is the right place to start. The goal is an outline of the tasks and responsibilities of each team member.

Even a complete outline of steps and tasks is not yet a project plan. The classic adage in project management is "time, quality, and cost -- pick any two." At best, an outline of tasks tells us something about project quality or scope. Until it's bounded with time and resources, however, we don't know whether we have a feasible project. A calendar and a list of available resources (people, tools, knowledge, money, space) will help us figure out if we can get an answer by a deadline and for a cost where the answer remains worth having.

To figure out how to break down a project into component parts and to outline them is difficult enough. If there are any significant uncertainties about tasks, resources, or deadlines it is not a deterministic problem. There may be a range of possible answers; there won't be a "right" answer. Multiply this by the multitude of proposed and ongoing projects within the typical enterprise and it's a wonder that organizations manage to do anything new.

In reflecting on his time as a general, Dwight Eisenhower once said, "in preparing for battle, plans are useless, but planning is indispensable." The stakes within organizations aren't as grave. However, the fundamental truth remains that we must make plans if we want to make informed tradeoffs among the competing claims for our attention and our budgets. Once we commit to a project, we aren't excused from periodically reassessing its continuing relevance and demands. Inexperienced project managers get upset as the real world upends their carefully drawn plans. Project managers that survive worry when everything is going according to plan.

During project execution, the plan helps you understand whether you are getting the resources that you expected, whether those resources are delivering in line with your expectations, and whether the actual tasks and dependencies match the tasks you anticipated. More importantly, though, you end up managing a constantly evolving collection of issues to be addressed and resolved. These can range from dealing with the problem of a promised expert resource not being available to the problem of a software tool performing more slowly than expected or failing under conditions that are likely to occur regularly rather than rarely.

Throughout the project, an individual, identifiable, project manager needs to take responsibility for establishing and maintaining the project team's and the organization's focus on working through the tasks and the issues needed to put a new way of working into practice.

Program Management—Coordinating Multiple Projects

Beyond the challenge of managing any individual project, there is the organizational challenge of managing resource contention, constraints, and issues across multiple competing projects. Formal organizational structures are designed to limit or eliminate the problems that arise in the context of routine operations. Job descriptions, headcount controls, policies, and procedures are all designed to match capacity against demand.

The inevitable uncertainties of project work are built in; they cannot be managed in any satisfactory way within conventional organizations. In most cases, these conflicts are routinely dealt with on an ad hoc basis; the parties involved take their complaints and pleas to a higher authority in the organization and hope for a favorable response. Absent the right disciplines, problem resolution, such as it is, becomes a function of favors returned for favors past, the persuasiveness of individual managers, and the politics of organizational power and influence. These predictable conflicts are best resolved with plans that are as explicit, transparent, specific, and concrete as possible.

In some more advanced organizations, project management dilemmas are addressed in an explicit and disciplined way. The tools and disciplines that work for individual projects are translated up a level where a group of presumably more senior managers with broader perspectives hammer out explicit tradeoffs between projects in terms of plans, resources, and budgets. At this level, organizations begin to talk of program management in a way that is analogous to project management.

Managing across multiple projects typically involves managing resource contention and issues that cross project boundaries in one way or another. Resource contention might surface in terms of a functional expert or subject matter expert being stretched too thinly across multiple projects or torn between project responsibilities and their departmental demands. If fifteen projects each assume a ten percent time commitment from the manager of inventory control, there is going to be a problem.

"Issue" is a necessarily loose notion for a question, problem, or opportunity that cannot be resolved within the confines of a single project. Two project teams working on different information systems, for example, might each presume a slightly different design for a new customer database. If this discrepancy is identified early, it can be resolved with a joint working session between the two teams. If it is missed or overlooked, the "issue" can morph into a major problem.

A steering committee composed of managers, with the necessary scope and perspective to make informed tradeoffs across projects, can best address resource contention and issue management. A reasonably standardized package of information maintained for each project and a centralized location or system for tracking issues will also be helpful.

A project information package should include a work plan, business case, timeline, project team organization, and budget. To support useful status reporting to the steering committee, the organization will need some way to track actual expenditures against budget and, more importantly, a way to track people's time against their project commitments. Often, when multiple projects are in flight the resident expert is expected to contribute ten percent of her time to a dozen projects while still doing her day job. Projects will flounder absent some system to track these resource contention issues.

While having no ability to monitor and track projects presents a significant organizational risk, there is a corresponding danger of over-investing in project management overhead. Too much bureaucracy will quickly transform project status reports into works of fiction. The project steering committee will also determine when to make progress on projects versus when to keep the current business operating smoothly.

Issue management is one of the simple tools for managing many, if not most, of the tradeoffs that surface across multiple projects. Projects necessarily stumble across multiple boundaries in any organization. The purpose of issue management is to identify and address the places where the current set of organizational processes and functions are conflicting. Visibility is the first step in working through an issue to come to an acceptable resolution.

Issues surface because some design choices and process options do not have a necessarily right answer. For project teams to formulate an answer, the issue first needs to be named, described, analyzed, and debated. An answer may require compromises from multiple parts of the system as a whole. These compromises need to be explicitly stated and the rationales identified so that they do not get lost in the mists of organizational history. Otherwise, it will be difficult to determine whether a new local improvement might compromise the entire system in the future. A systematic process and organizational practice of working through issues results in better systems tradeoffs now and provides critical context for future tradeoffs.

The mechanics of coordinating multiple projects into a coherent transformation program are an important element. Ultimately, these mechanics only matter when they provide a basis for senior management to assess and work through the key issues and tradeoffs as they occur. A clearly defined and identified steering committee of top managers must be created to do this work.

This steering committee will meet and interact frequently; at least weekly and, at peak times, even daily. The steering committee exists to resolve those issues that cannot be dealt with within the boundaries of an individual project. Sound project plans, good issue management, and focusing meetings on decisions instead of analysis all contribute to making the most effective use of the committee's perspective and experience.

Connecting Project to Change Management

Projects are the primary building blocks of change management. Change management is about taking the organization, its functions, and processes from today's stable configuration to a new stable configuration that creates a better and more profitable fit between the organization and its competitive environment. Projects break that journey into more manageable chunks.

Projects are also the place where the project team learns to understand and commit to the new organizational reality. If the organizational goal is to have everyone come to understand and commit to the project, then you want to take advantage of these project efforts in pursuit of that goal.

There will always be people who are resistant to the changes that are occurring within an organization. Some will be people in roles that are being diminished by the changes taking place. Others will be people threatened by the general increase in uncertainty and ambiguity. Understanding the specific anxieties and concerns of those voicing or demonstrating resistance is essential to craft the most effective responses. For example, engineers or sales reps who are anxious about how their deep and hard-won knowledge of products and customers will remain relevant in a new order need to be managed differently than those whose power and influence are linked to some idiosyncrasy of a now obsolete internal process. The first group may have critical responsibilities in the new regime and need to be educated on how they will operate and prosper within the new system. The second group may need to clearly understand that their future depends on how diligently they work to bring new practices and processes to fruition. Their place in a new system may well be uncertain. The leadership task is to be absolutely clear that the old system is gone.

Managers' instincts to seek efficiencies can work against the broader goal of long-term effectiveness. Examined in isolation project activities appear to be "extra" work; for they are perceived to divert attention from the primary work of the organization. Additionally, projects disrupt the emotional comfort that people derive from their daily routines. Consequently, managers are tempted to staff projects thinly and to use outside resources to complete project tasks.

This approach misses the larger goal of moving the organization to a new normal. The business goals of these projects have not been met until personnel have learned about and settled into the new processes and functions. Personnel aren't settled into the new normal until it has become habit and has displaced old habits.

Part of putting new ways of working into practice is to make it difficult or impossible for users to access the old ways. One telling example occurred shortly after ITW acquired Signode when the president of ITW back in 1986 visited Signode's data center housing the computers and support staff running all of Signode's operations. Reportedly, when the president of ITW saw the large computer room and the assembled technology staff, he announced that he would return in 90 days to pull the plug on the center and shut it down. The senior technology manager politely stated, "Perhaps you don't understand. This data center runs the entire company; you CAN'T unplug it." The President's response was "No, you don't understand. I am coming back in 90 days and turning this computer off - figure out how to run your business without it." ITW's president set into motion the break up of Signode into 100 different, smaller companies. For the president of ITW – it was about forcing change and removing the tools that people needed to continue to run the company as they had previously.

Breaking away from the old is as important as learning the new and can manifest itself in multiple ways. For example, some steps to implement ways to manage programs;

- Project Planners are released or reassigned.

- ERP systems are dismantled and replaced with visual systems

- Standing meetings are replaced with the daily walk.

- Functional job classifications are eliminated and cell leaders are assigned.

- Inventory triggers are changed and the computer systems used to run the Company are dismantled as business metrics are posted and made visual.

To achieve business goals, engage as many people as possible as soon as possible to create the new normal. Best utilize outside resources to maintain the old processes while the in-house staff learns new routines to let go of old methods. People will hide the fact that they are holding onto old systems.

For example, after converting a recently acquired company to fit into the Kanban system we were running, we discovered an engineer who had quietly kept a forecast system in his desk believing that the pull through system would break down and he was worried that the company would run out of product. Unfortunately, this engineer was spending a lot of time recording and managing the forecast system rather than making certain that the pull through system was functioning. It was only after the engineer was required to turn over all the paperwork and files supporting his forecast system that he was able to focus on and learn to use the Kanban pull through system as designed.

This was not a failure on the part of the engineer. It was a failure on the part of the project team for ignoring the broader goal of the change effort. The Kanban system's design was already complete. The project team's task was to integrate the acquisition into the existing system; a trivial task on paper only. The challenge was to get people to understand the new system and to adopt new habits. The project team's responsibility was to look for and discover the old practices that the organization was holding on to.

However, this failure may have also reflected a lack of support from senior management. Perhaps management was more focused on ticking off the details of the project plan than on moving the organization to a new normal. Management support is the "secret sauce" of successful organizational change. With management support, projects succeed; without it, projects flounder and fail.

Missing or inadequate support is typically easier to recognize. In one company, a previous effort to implement a Kanban system was viewed as a failure. The failure occurred because no one stressed or enforced the discipline of using the Kanban system as designed. The organization interpreted the implementation failure as an indictment of the Kanban technique. As we attempted to implement Kanban again, workers on the floor operated outside the design of the Kanban system. Some workers would turn in their Kanban cards early (before they were actually out of inventory in a bin) trying to ensure they had inventory. Other workers were holding on to cards because they felt the movement of the product was too sporadic to justify the quantities being held in inventory. Workers were making these decisions with the best of intentions. Workers' efforts to outperform the Kanban system were undermining its integrity instead. We added extra education to explain not only the mechanical details of the Kanban system but the underlying logic as well. Ultimately, one employee did need to be disciplined, but everyone eventually grasped the logic and the mechanics and the system performed as designed.

To get everyone in the system to commit to the new habits that are necessary it is essential that they understand how these systems work as a whole to accomplish the goals of the organization. The simplest way to convey how the systems work is to engage people, as widely as possible, in designing and implementing the new systems. The benefits you gain in buy-in, commitment to change, and understanding that flow from involvement in the transition from the outset far outweigh the short terms costs in "efficiency" in doing the analyses and project execution themselves.

Typical 80/20 Project Time Line

A typical 80/20 analysis project (Exhibit 31) from start to finish will take about three months to develop. Executing the change is more dependent on the individual business. Often the execution stage can take another four to six months to get the basic systems in place. The execution of the transfer from one system to the next can be very challenging. The key to a successful transition is to have exceptionally strong project management skills.

After the transition, the culture needs to shift from change management to continuous improvement.

Exhibit 31
80/20 Analysis Project Timeline (typical)

Data Dump   1-2 days

Red Light/Green Light Analysis	1 weeks
Quad Generation	1 weeks
Product Line Simplification	2 week
Economic Modeling	1 weeks
Evaluation of Quads	2 weeks
Exploring Toolkit Alternatives	2 weeks
Developing implementation plan	3 weeks
Total Time	3 months
Executing Implementation Plan	4-6 months

This is given 1-2 project leads to manage the project through an organization with the functional managers participating in critical meetings during the week. The standard of success is that none of your customers know that you have actually changed your manufacturing process. This is considered success. There will be problems. You need to anticipate and manage them as much as possible.

In one transformation, as we shifted from a forecast purchase system to a visual pull through system, we had to truck in chemicals on an expedited basis to maintain continual flow through the plant. The cost of this single expedited delivery was $200. Some of the skeptics offered this as an example of system failure. The Kanban level for this chemical was adjusted and the problem never recurred. Given that this was the only significant issue that occurred during the transformation and never repeated, this was a successful effort.

CHAPTER 15
THE IMPROVEMENT CYCLE–
INSTITUTIONALIZING THE PROCESS

In this chapter we turn to this question of how to strike a dynamic balance between stability and change. We will examine how to institutionalize the improvement process to sustain change. We will examine how to make our organizations living systems that continue to grow and evolve as 80/20 organizations.

Stepping back from the analytical process and the individual improvement tools we have been discussing, there is an underlying theory of improvement driving our approach. A cycle of improvement isn't complete until the organization delivers consistent, repeatable, results from a new process or practice. A New Year's resolution to get more exercise isn't successful until you wake up one morning in April in your exercise outfit halfway down the block and can't quite remember how you got there.

Change and change management has typically been treated as a rare, short event separating long periods of stability (Kaizen). We no longer live in that world, either as individuals or organizations. It is indeed a world of "permanent white water" and longing for a time when it wasn't is time wasted.

The first time that an organization works through the process we have described will not be its last. Organizations must think in terms of how to incorporate continuous improvement and change into their overall systems. Companies must ask, "What is the likely useful life of a process or an information system?" "How long do we invest in patching and maintaining the old versus when do we move to something new?"

Change—Rationale, Rehearsal, Reflection, Repetition

The change process we have described is also a learning process that individuals and organizations must go through. First, understand the basic rationale for change and then proceed to rehearse new methods and practices. Next, reflect on the results and tune the details. Finally, repeat the process until new practices reach the point where they are habitual and automatic.

This cycle of rationale, rehearsal, reflection, and repetition has to be completed before we see meaningful and sustainable results, whether we are talking about personal habits or new production processes. As individuals, awareness of the cycle makes learning more manageable and the inevitable setbacks and frustrations more understandable.

Things are more complicated within organizations. Organizations can't stop current operations and activities while everyone works through the learning cycle at their own pace. A continual change process must balance the need to keep the organization operating effectively with the disruptions of learning and internalizing new ways of working. If management emphasizes predicting and controlling current operations the change effort stalls because it never reaches critical mass. Contrarily, if management emphasizes leaping forward to try new opportunities and improvements they risk creating an organization that never stabilizes enough to meet customers' needs

Most organizations are content to muddle along, to pretend that the world is stable, and to rely on natural human capacities to learn and adapt. If the world is indeed stable and change is both incremental and slow, this strategy can work. We don't recommend this strategy for the world that we see. Let's consider each of these four stages in turn and ask how we might balance efficiency and effectiveness, today's realities and tomorrow's possibilities, in a more manageable way.

RATIONALE FOR CHANGE—INSIGHT GOES TO THE ANALYST

Change always starts with an argument that there has to be a better way. In the mythology of the solo American inventor and entrepreneur, it is the tale of the "better mousetrap." Passion and conviction can carry the individual a long way in the absence of analysis and supporting evidence. Many successful entrepreneurs built their businesses on thin evidence. Our conviction is that evidence and analysis are key elements of a better process to improve organizational performance.

80/20 analyses and quadrant reviews shape and organize the arguments for where to best focus attention and resources. The 80/20 rule separates what is important from what is not. Quad maps push that further to reveal the economic core of best products and best customers. Organizing the data contained in a company's own information systems provides a factual counterweight to the opinions of those who "know better." There are always surprises in the analysis process, discoveries of "things we know that just aren't so." Those inclined to hold onto those "things we know that just aren't so" frequently sit in positions of authority and influence in the organization. Regardless of where they sit in the organization they, like all of us, will hold onto their beliefs in spite of contradictory evidence.

The transformation process and the management of change from old ways to new ways can be very difficult because you have to make certain that key functions such as purchasing, production triggers, and customers' orders are met in a fluid manner.

This is a fundamental characteristic of the human brain. We need to account for this when designing effective change efforts. Our recommendation and practice is to identify those key individuals who will need to accept the evidence and analysis and to involve them directly in the early analytical stages of developing the 80/20 analyses and quadrant reviews.

Accepting the results and implications of an 80/20 review is both an intellectual and an emotional task. Insight, acceptance, and commitment to the evidence are all built through the process of digging out, filtering, organizing, and interpreting the data. Reviewing the results at the end of the effort is rarely sufficient.

Our shorthand for this phenomenon is that **"insight goes to the analyst."**

Don't be overly concerned with the real or perceived efficiency of the analysis process. The mechanics of the analysis make it tempting to offload it to junior analysts and staff. Given the staff's relative skill and comfort with the basic analytical tools of the trade, this approach is understandable and some of that skill base is, in fact, necessary. But this is neither the time nor the place to worry about issues of staff productivity or efficiency. The important output of the analytical phase is insight and comprehension. Engaging key senior level people to actively guide and shape the analysis yields a twofold advantage. First, senior management's experience compared to junior staff can guide the analysis to deeper levels of insight and understanding. More importantly, senior management's substantive involvement from the outset ensures that key players will understand and buy into the analytical insights and outcomes on both an intellectual and emotional basis.

REHEARSAL AND REFLECTION

We label the next steps in our approach to change as "rehearsal" and "reflection." The order here is arbitrary and is merely a convenience for presentation purposes. In the real world, nothing is ever as straightforward or linear as any of the simplifying maps might suggest. The analytical process produces an agenda for change that identifies the scale and scope of multiple opportunities and the various improvement tools and techniques highlight the path to a possible new future. The players must learn their new roles and new lines, practice them, and become comfortable with them. The new sets and lights have to be designed and built, and the players need to become comfortable performing in their new space. Through it all, they need the opportunity to step back from the detail and reflect on what is going on and how it continues to evolve.

A level of messiness is an essential feature in shifting from today's familiar but underperforming environment to the new normal that exists initially as only potential. Messiness can be especially uncomfortable to both workers and managers who relish the seeming precision and predictability of smoothly run operations. We use the word "seeming" here quite deliberately. The reality in most organizations is that even the best run operations appear precise and predictable only at a distance. Up close these systems have a full complement of shortcuts, workarounds, and tricks of the trade that let them function in the face of the day-to-day unpredictability that is the real world.

Forgetting the inescapable messiness of reality is a path to embarrassing decisions.

As an example, one manufacturing operation sought to outsource the production of a portion of its components. The company negotiated a contract that promised excellent cost savings and the engineering drawings were shipped off to the sub-contractor. A few weeks later the outsourced components arrived and flowed into the larger production process. One hundred percent of the components were rejected in production.

Inspection revealed that every component had been built precisely as specified in the engineering drawings. The next level of analysis revealed that none of the components manufactured in house conformed to the engineering drawings. Production staff on the floor had learned the adjustments necessary to make the components actually work but none of those adjustments were recorded in the engineering drawings.

This example is not unique. All real organizations operate this way. Anyone who believes otherwise is naive or willfully blind. To move an organization from a system that works to a new system that works management has to account for and allow the time for the necessary rich mix of technology, processes, practices, and work-arounds to form and coalesce before the benefits identified during analysis can appear.

When management embarks on change evolution will occur. Rehearsal and reflection have to occur before the organizational system can reach its full performance potential. Acknowledge that adaptation happens, anticipate it, account for it, and incorporate it in your planning and in your plans. Organizations value precision and predictability. Change is neither. Organizations that deny or struggle with the messiness and unpredictability of change might temporarily suppress or postpone change, but they cannot prevent it. Better to build that into the change cycle than have it occur later.

REPETITION

Eventually this evolutionary learning and change process becomes more about consistent repetition and less about inventing the new. In today's "permanent whitewater" environment, however, steady state is not sharply delineated from more volatile states nor is there any guarantee how long any state will persist. Management must now make an explicit and conscious choice of how closely, precisely, and frequently they wish to monitor organizational performance relative to their expectations of steady state.

Work processes can be monitored in multiple ways including:

- Activities and resource consumption.

- Quantity and quality of outputs.

- Labor productivity.

- Asset productivity.

- Error rates.

Targets for any of these metrics can be set based on the design of the process and actual behavior monitored relative to those targets. In a steady state environment, variances from target indicate that the process is out of conformance with the design and some corrective action is required. Sophisticated organizations might account for a learning curve before actual metrics meet their targets. Still more sophisticated organizations might also account for an ongoing learning improvement based on total cumulative output over time.

A permanent whitewater world makes variance analysis significantly more complicated. In this environment, variances might result not only from how well a process conforms to design, but also from changes in the external environment that might demand a re-evaluation and re-design of the process.

Seeding a Data Driven Decision Culture

Over 35 years ago, Jim was sitting in an office overlooking 54th Street and Sixth Avenue in New York City. Jim was sufficiently naïve and ignorant to believe that he was on the Avenue of the Americas because that was what the sign said on the corner. This was an early encounter with the contradiction between the official and insider versions of reality. The office belonged to Reginald Jones, a patrician graduate of Princeton, who ran Arthur Andersen's New York consulting practice. Jones explained how the information systems of the day made it possible for companies to break out their budgets so that each manager of each department in an organization could get a picture of their piece of turf and how it performed against plan. Each manager could manage against a discrete responsibility report and all of the reports could be consolidated into a single picture of the organization as a whole.

The headquarters of IT&T were across the street and CEO Harold Geneen[13] was using just such a system to turn the screws on his managers. This was a world of predictability and stability. The conceptual elegance of responsibility reporting was well matched to a time when CEOs like Geneen were routinely compared to captains of ocean liners, aircraft carriers, and oil tankers.

Today's technologists speak of data cubes, balanced scorecards, and dashboards but the underlying logic remains the same. Carve things up to assign accountability to discrete individuals. Deliver reports to these individuals that provide an accurate picture of their corner of the world. Produce the reports rapidly enough and accurately enough that managers can understand why actual performance doesn't match the plan and do something useful with that understanding. We keep hoping that the next round of technology and clever software will finally crack the case.

We dodge the question of where are the limits that make managerial judgment a continuing necessity in most organizations and most business environments. The boundaries between the decision problems we can solve and the ones we can't shift regularly enough that we can price every individual seat on a flight between Chicago and New York and simultaneously crash the world economy because bankers can take positions on mortgage backed securities that have no discernible connection to any economic reality.

The issue is a two cultures problem. On one extreme are the decision theorists; analytically inclined children of the Enlightenment seeking truth. They seek patterns in the data that conclusively point to right answers. Bad answers and bad outcomes represent failures of theory and failures of analysis. We don't have the right data, or the right model. Better data (more accurate, more timely, more detailed) and better models (more robust, more predictive, more insightful) will tell us which channel, which market, which customer, which price is right. No judgment need apply once the model has been created and vetted.

On the other extreme, decisions are a function of organizational power and influence. Data and models are relevant primarily in terms of whether they provide defensible support for the decisions we advocate based on judgment and experience. Managers and executives operate in the corridors of power. If we hold onto power, then by definition our decisions have been good. In the worst case, our analyses ratify decisions that have already been made.

With real decisions in real organizations, answers lie in the gray between the poles of algorithmic certainty and political power. In Samuel Butler's observation, "life is the art of drawing sufficient conclusions from insufficient premises." Think of the relation between data and decisions as a continuum ranging from analytical certainty to instinctive judgment. We can divide that continuum into three regions:

- **Data determines the decision**. An underlying model exists that links data and decisions; provide quality data and decisions become deterministic. Airline revenue yield models and inventory replenishment models are the classic examples. There is an invention challenge to build and vet a good model and there is an ongoing data management problem to collect the necessary data at the right levels of quality and timeliness. But there is little in the way of a managerial problem.

- **Data and management judgment vie for dominance**. Here the models and data may still be in flux. They may be new in general or new to a particular organization. They introduce a risk of putting existing managerial judgments in question. In this realm the challenges are both analytic and political. The models must be proven and the quality and availability of the data established. At the same time, the potential impact of new decision processes needs to be evaluated and assessed.

- **Data informs management judgment**. Strategic management problems fall in this realm. For these decisions as much or more time needs to be devoted to formulating the questions and teasing out the models as in gathering and vetting the data. Data analysis by itself will not reveal the best management decision. Done well, good data, models, and analysis can put useful boundaries on the decision problem and inform management where the most troubling risks and issues to be managed lie.

We clearly belong in the school that prefers decisions grounded in data. However analytically correct or defensible these decisions might be, success or failure ultimately depends on the organization's ability to go from decision to execution consistently and effectively. We also believe that organizations can cultivate and develop the skills necessary to analyze the data and to consequently make decisions to execute effective change.

Becoming an 80/20 Culture

One of ITW's advantages over other companies is that ITW has a culture that embraces this entire philosophy. They have proven, much like the U.S. Marine Corps, that they can take any organization and successfully transform it into a new, lean manufacturing machine. Changing the culture of your company to embrace these concepts will be more difficult. Many of the participants will go along believing it is another intellectual exercise to be endured until the CEO goes on to the next one. These tend to be the individuals who are most resistant to change and who will point out every single problem.

After an acquisition, ITW allows the new company about a year to transform. Companies were put through a series of steps to get the business's owners and managers to understand the system. As a part of the financial audits, ITW also does an 80/20 audit reviewing and ranking how business are doing according to the principles and practices.

After the initial 80/20 project it is most helpful to come back to the line simplification process as a part of the annual review. Businesses should be expected to have a thorough review of the business and explain how they are driving their business towards their Quad 1. The annual review process tends to be a great place to reinforce the new culture.

Often we have found that people on the plant floor better understand the types of systems we are trying to set-up. These individuals are called out and used as examples for the rest of the organization. This mentoring process tends to help develop buy in.

Best Practices meetings can be particularly helpful when you call out people for a particular practice and/or implementation of the principles. Giving people public acknowledgement and allowing them to explain what and how they accomplished one of the key items in the toolkit can be transformative in an organization.

There are many excellent videos and training materials that can be used to stimulate discussions of practices and policies. Regular reviews and discussions of the ideas and beliefs reinforce learning and uptake. If you pick one of the items in the toolkit and discuss the concept., this can generate ideas about how to make it better on the plant floor.

CHAPTER 16
MIP CASE STUDY

MIP was started in 1987, manufacturing hand tools and equipment and selling primarily through distribution and catalog companies. It had a variety of customers, all resellers, including packaging companies, catalog companies, paper houses and industrial supply houses.

GENERAL BACKGROUND

- Company had a standard product offering—but also had branched out into ancillary tools and equipment that could be sold through this distribution channel.

- Company was started in Chicago and then slowly expanded outside to the entire US market and then overseas. Items that the company manufactured were sold into the international market.

- 60% of the product offering was manufactured—the rest was imported and resold across the country and the world.

- Single location company, sole owner.

FOCUS OF COMPANY

- Middle market company, value oriented, broad offering of product within niche space.

- Excellent customer service within niche space.

- Heavy focus on engineering and new product development.

- Production planning was accomplished with the use of material resource planning.

- Safety stock, functional layout of machining, and several large assembly tables.

- Products were made-to-stock.

FINANCIALS

- Sales of approximately $6 to $7 Million.

- Gross margin of around 40%.

- Operating profit of around 4%.

- 52 employees.

- Heavy debt load, inventory turning over around 4 times a year.

OPERATIONS

- The number of daily transactions and one-touches in the company were exceptionally high.

- Company was often out of parts requiring everyone to jump through multiple hoops to get orders shipped.

- Excessive material handling due to the need to collect parts from a supermarket mentality to bring to production and/or assembly.

- Excessive finished goods inventory but with high variability. Some tools we had a lot of and others we had very little.

- Significant amount of repetitive machine set-ups and breakdowns.

- Large QC infrastructure built into the system in an attempt to guarantee quality.

- Large amount of management focus on the expediting and management of parts.

COMPANY STATE PRIOR TO ACQUISITION

- Company was already in a space acquirer knew well.

- It was in a market position acquirer currently didn't occupy (Value Proposition).

- Sales structure was geographically organized rather than customer centric.

- Pricing discipline didn't exist nor was it enforced. Special deals and one-offs for customers added to the overall complexity.

- 100's of vendors—low cost providers almost always received business.

- Management of cash flow impacted a lot of the decisions.

- Inventory was high—but the company would still run out of parts and be unable to produce.

- Enormous amount of transactions and complexity.

COMPANY ACQUIRED

- Mentor was appointed to help company to facilitate the process.

- Plant tours of converted companies were frequent and included all levels of management and some line personnel.

- Company and management were initially very skeptical of the 80/20 process.

- Typical objections—It will never work here, they don't understand our business, our business is too random.

UNDERSTANDING AND CHANGE STARTED AT THE TOP

- Decision made to embrace the change.

- Middle management initially was not on board—but embraced the process with the understanding that if they wanted to remain in control, then they had better take control of the process.

PROCESS WAS AS FOLLOWS

- Red/Light Green Light Analysis.

- Quad Analysis.

- Line simplification.

- Application of Toolkit.

- Implementation Plan—Short Term (3 months), Long Term (12 months).

DATA ANALYSIS

- Direct Margin/Gross Margin was used at the key driver for the analysis.

- Data Dump was generated.

- General Manager performed initial analytical review.

WORKING THROUGH THE DATA

- Initial Data Dump of information.

- Sort the data in the Red/Green Light Analysis—started to pick up on some general basic themes, shared this with other management.

- Understand the data from a Quad perspective.

RED LIGHT/GREEN LIGHT

- Customer and Vendor sort were classic 80/20—actually proving out to be 90/10 in most cases.

- 10 core manufactured products that made up most of our revenue stream.

- 30 core customers that made up most of our revenue stream.

- Pricing and focus was all over the place with non-critical customers constantly adding complexity to our manufacturing process and then not supporting this through pricing.

- Red Light/Green Light provided platform for discussion of business leaders. Helped people better understand the process, participate, and buy into it.

QUAD PROCESS

- Quad Process was used to analyze the business from a variety of perspectives - but it specifically focused around the data.

- Quad Analysis revealed several different types of customers: Stocking Distributors, Catalog Companies, Non-Stocking Distributors, and Distributors using the business as a warehouse.

- There was a very large quantity of Quad 3 Customers, as well as Quad 4 Customers and Products.

PRODUCT LINE SIMPLIFICATION

- Eliminated products lines, parts, tools, and equipment. Cut product offering from several thousand down to a couple hundred.

- This involved working closely with the sales team to determine non-impactful elimination (Quad 2 and Quad 4).

- Eliminated almost all ancillary product including Parts for Imported, Economy Tools, Knives, Semi-Automatic Strapping Machines, Kraft Paper Dispensers, Label Dispensers.

- Worked hard not to just to say no to customers—provided non-competitive alternative sources, made several last-time buys to keep customers happy, trained customer service to manage customer's expectations.

- Minimal impact to Gross Margin. Huge simplification of the business.

IMPLEMENTATION PLAN

- With the product line simplification complete, was then able to step back from the business and return to the toolkit.

SEVERAL ITEMS IN THE TOOLKIT WERE CRITICAL TO REDEFINING THE NEW SIMPLER BUSINESS.

- Pull-through manufacturing rather than push.

- Kanban System set-up for both finished goods and all critical parts.

- In-lining process defined and established.

- Dedicated equipment and simplification of the manufacturing process.

CRITICAL STEPS

- Master list of products to be eliminated and the process on how best to handle was established.

- Pricing review and the initiation of pricing discipline was established based on Quads (Quad 4 customers had to pay standard pricing, Quad 3 customers were slowly transitioned over to the standard price list.

- Floor transformation plan was put in place to in-line Quad 1 products.

- Inventory Kanbans were calculated and a system put in place to set-up the visual systems.

- Vendor reduction program was started and vendors started to establish a Rolling Purchase Order System.

- Evaluated business looking for opportunities to eliminate transactions.

ADDITIONAL SIMPLIFICATION EFFORTS

- Quad 2 products were grouped together and separated on the plant floor. Manufacturing cells were set up and designed to focus on short runs over varying products.

- Quad 4 products were eliminated over time.

- Engineering took the time to focus on simplification/consolidating of raw materials and the simplification of the assembly process rather than chasing the new revenue dollars.

IMPLEMENTATION

- Process included a 3-month review of the data and development of an implementation plan.

- During this time management and plant floor personnel were educated on the 80/20 process. Much of this was done by touring other facilities.

- Implementation process was reviewed by assigned Mentor and Group Vice President.

DIFFICULTIES

- Not all managers were on board with the new path—a lot of doubts.

- Training in new roles took time - especially training the vendors on the process and the flow.

- Tool and equipment had to be made to streamline operations.

OPERATIONAL OUTCOME

- Complexity in the organization was significantly reduced.

- Culture of autonomy and ownership was pushed out to the plant floor.

- Quad 1 Customers felt more focus and attention. Turning over of Quad 4 Customers further strengthened Quad 1 Customers.

- Employees were happier and less harried because we had the product to ship to our customers.

- Management of the company went from computer report driving to a visual system.

FINANCIAL OUTCOME

- Revenue remained flat for the first year—but then took off in the second year as the focus became on the Quad 1 Customers.

- Operating Income went from 4% when owner operated to 12% the first year and then peaking at 28% 7 years later.

- Inventory turns went from 3.5 to 12 times per year.

- Increased revenue per employee from $137,000 to $425,000.

- Customer fill rates improved dramatically.

BUSINESS MANAGEMENT

- Company became easier to run, so more time became available to look for new opportunities.

- Conducted 80/20 review once a year as part of the annual budgeting process.

- Discovery that we were our own masters of our destiny.

- You can always learn better ways to improve and run a business.

- MIP held up as the poster child of successful transformation within the Packaging Division.

PART 5
APPENDICES

APPENDIX 1—GLOSSARY

Backwash Analysis – Historical Sales Data is run back over the Finished Goods Kanban Levels to see the number of times the operation would have run out of stock.

C-class inventory - inexpensive, secondary items that are readily available from an outside source and generally have short lead times. They are treated differently than regular inventory and tend to be expensed when they are received.

Cost accounting system – collection, analysis, and evaluation of information involving costs. Typically these are indirect costs and there is a process or technique employed in allocating them amongst the products and/or services.

Data dump - colloquial term for the retrieval of four main types of company data (products, customers, transactions and vendors), which are then downloaded into four spreadsheets. This process happens before data analysis begins.

Decentralization – the process of shifting power away from a central governing body and dispersing it across multiple smaller units. For instance, corporations with multiple branches may give the managers at these branches more power. This also applies to planning process for companies and organizations.

Dedicated equipment – Production facilities and equipment that has been dedicated to a specific and/or single operation and product group working to eliminate the set-up and change over.

Enterprise Resource Planning Systems (ERP) - integrate internal and external management information across an entire organization, embracing finance/accounting, manufacturing, sales and service, customer relationship management.

Gemba walk – derived from the Japanese word Gemba (meaning "real place"); refers to a daily walk through an organization in which the core functional leaders check each of the major departments to ensure smooth running of daily operations.

Gross margin - difference between a product's revenue and direct material, plus direct labor, and indirect expenses.

In-lining – the process of organizing the production flow in such a way that each sequential step takes place in a single unidirectional flow going from the beginning of assembly to the packaging of the final product.

Kaizen event – represents a conscious effort to make improvements in a company through the collective strength of a focused team working in a specific area over a short time frame. Kaizen literally translates as "change for the better."

Kanban system - generally refers to a two-bin system used to guide the manufacturing process and ensure a constant flow of products to minimize shortages. In some cases, 3-5 bins can be used instead of 2 bins.

Lean manufacturing - a production practice that considers spending resources for any goal besides creating value for the end customer to be wasteful, and therefore important to eliminate. The principle is heavily influenced by the Toyota Production System.

Line simplification - acronym for product line simplification; the reduction of the number of products in a product line that occurs as a direct result of the quad analysis.

OEM - acronym for original equipment manufacturer; an organization that serves as the original manufacturer of products purchased by another company and retailed under that company's name.

One-at-a-time manufacturing – creating a product from start to finish but only making one, rather than in batches.

Outsourcing – obtaining products or services from an outside source, rather than internally.

Pareto Principle - refers to an 80/20 distribution. When applied to business, 80 percent of profit comes from 20 percent of customers or products.

Point of use – the location within a plant where items or personnel are used.

Pull-through production rate – also known as a pull-through system. This is a system in which a company and/or organization manufactures product only when they sell a product. When you sell a product, you make a product.

Quad analysis – a process for breaking down your customers and products into a four part classification system based on where they are on the 80/20 rule.

Quad map - summary system of the Quad Process showing the outcome from the Quad Analysis.

QC - acronym for quality control; process in which companies review the quality of all aspects of production.

Red light/green light analysis – the first stage of data analysis after the data dump in which the Pareto principle is applied and data is sorted and placed into specific classifications.

Rolling purchase order system – technique used to streamline the purchasing of items being used continuously.

Silos – management systems that cannot exchange information with other related systems in an organization.

SMED - acronym for single minute exchange of a die; a lean manufacturing strategy used to minimize the time lost during a changeover.

Six sigma – a business management system, pioneered by Motorola, that aims to improve the quality of process outputs by identifying and removing defects and minimizing variability in processes.

SKU - acronym for stock keeping unit; the number or code that is used to identify company products

Toolkit – a set of business strategies that collectively define the way a company operates.

Transaction analysis – study of transaction patterns within a business

Triad structure – the three-part departmental structure that is typical of many organizations; comprised of operations, shipping and receiving/warehouse and customer service/sales.

Value stream mapping – a lean manufacturing technique used to analyze and design the flow of materials and information required to bring a product or service to a consumer.

Vendor consolidation – the reduction and management of vendors that can occur as a result of the 80/20 process.

vendor managed inventory (VMI) system – system in which the vendor plays a key role in inventory planning for the customer.

WIP - Acronym for work-in process, representing an inventory stage

APPENDIX 2—MECHANICS OF 80/20 AND QUAD ANALYSIS

You need to create three files by extracting information from your accounting system. Data is extracted for both Product and Customer and then the Transaction File in order to perform your 80/20 analysis and build your quad map.

These files with relevant data fields are listed below:

Data Dump Product:

Product #,

Product Description,

Last 12 Months Revenue,

Gross Margin,

Gross Margin %,

Quantity Sold; 12-24 Months,

Revenue,

Gross Margin,

Quantity Sold;

Current Inventory, (average inventory if you have it, if not beginning inventory),

Product Grouping/Industry Segment Class.

Data Dump Customer:

Customer #,

Customer Name,

Last 12 Months Revenue,

Gross Margin,

Gross Margin %.

Last 12-24 Months Revenue,

Gross Margin,

Customer Groupings, Industry Specifications if you have one.

Data Dump Transaction: (Consolidated Customer Transaction over the last 12 months showing)

Customer #,

Customer Name,

Product Number,

Product Name,

Revenue,

Gross Margin,

Quantity,

Product Grouping,

Customer Grouping.

In the product and customer dump we are looking 24 months back. The reason to include the second year is to make certain there haven't been major changes in product or customer. If there were a major shift you would want to include it in the analysis.

80/20 ANALYSIS OF THE CUSTOMER WORKSHEET

We'll use the customer worksheet to step through the mechanics of identifying the actual 80/20 distribution in an organization. The first step is to open the customer worksheet and sort customer sales from highest to lowest on Current Year Sales. Then, insert a new column, Cumulative Current Year Sales, to calculate a running total of Current Year Sales producing the following worksheet:

2
Add Cumulative
Sales Total

1
Sort by Sales
Highest to
Lowest

Customer Name	Current Year Quantity	Current Year Sales	Cumulative Current Year Sales	Current Year Cost of Goods Sold	Current Year Margin	Current Year Margin Percentage	Primary Plant Location	Sales Office Location
Ironey Distributors	23,560	7,416,966	7,416,966	6,025,561	1,391,405	18.76%	Fresno	Fresno
Doctrine Distibutors	20,715	4,698,480	12,115,446	3,310,586	1,387,894	29.54%	Tampa	Tampa
Conum Products	45,277	3,138,278	15,253,724	1,880,836	1,257,442	40.07%	Fresno	Fresno
IDS Industrial Products	18,060	3,049,999	18,303,723	1,239,795	1,810,204	59.35%	Tampa	Fresno
RC Megovern	21,423	2,103,678	20,407,401	1,226,227	877,451	41.71%	Houston	Houston
Kepemy	3,872	1,962,222	22,369,624	1,039,891	922,331	47.00%	Fresno	Fresno
Mega Widgets	8,054	1,657,655	24,027,278	1,338,765	318,890	19.24%	Tampa	Tampa
Micro Pentronics	9,623	1,637,893	25,665,171	1,352,230	285,663	17.44%	Tampa	Tampa
Total Industries	11,884	1,163,089	26,828,260	716,187	446,902	38.42%	Tampa	Tampa
Baxter Products	3,010	1,150,740	27,978,999	455,044	695,695	60.46%	Houston	Houston
Morgan Industies	2,746	1,128,424	29,107,424	300,097	828,327	73.41%	Tampa	Tampa
PC Technologies	1,823	656,203	29,763,627	240,256	415,947	63.39%	Houston	Houston
Funnel Spin	1,462	628,239	30,391,866	245,806	382,433	60.87%	Pittsburgh	Pittsburg
Ohio Lean Technologies	1,172	598,034	30,989,900	229,918	368,116	61.55%	Houston	Pittsburg
Cultural Data	2,133	569,666	31,559,565	199,775	369,891	64.93%	Houston	Tampa
Most Dytronics	2,539	493,204	32,052,769	152,220	340,984	69.14%	Houston	Houston
Cole Instruments	1,199	491,864	32,544,634	167,836	324,029	65.88%	Tampa	Tampa
Grainger Sales	1,066	389,658	32,934,292	141,613	248,046	63.66%	Tampa	Tampa
Soimin Sdn. Bhd.	1,109	313,516	33,247,808	186,570	126,946	40.49%	Houston	Tampa
Royal Beacon	1,233	287,775	33,535,582	144,684	143,091	49.72%	Houston	Houston
McMaster-Carr	681	283,375	33,818,957	112,842	170,533	60.18%	Tampa	Tampa
Sory Tall Grass	16,978	256,059	34,075,016	163,159	92,900	36.28%	Houston	Fresno
R.S. Hughes Distribution	784	253,178	34,328,194	82,418	170,761	67.45%	Tampa	Fresno
B. Royou Gmbh	631	218,442	34,546,636	77,615	140,827	64.47%	Houston	Tampa
BS Heffer Consolidated	412	208,598	34,755,234	88,385	120,213	57.63%	Fresno	Fresno
Phinster OY	275	208,023	34,963,257	83,569	124,454	59.83%	Houston	Houston
Showa Worldwide Sdn. Bhd.	384	192,505	35,155,762	76,466	116,039	60.28%	Tampa	Tampa
Botox Consolidated	1,355	188,426	35,344,188	43,680	144,745	76.82%	Fresno	Fresno
Monoprix	98,641	180,025	35,524,213	154,937	25,088	13.94%	Tampa	Tampa
Fuctional Products	819	179,246	35,703,460	62,530	116,716	65.11%	Tampa	Tampa
Memorial Widgets	669	177,943	35,881,402	55,787	122,155	68.65%	Houston	Houston
X-Z Products	412	176,881	36,058,283	59,407	117,475	66.41%	Tampa	Tampa
Brun Master	620	176,209	36,234,492	58,209	118,000	66.97%	Tampa	Tampa
Dobbies S.a.l.	2,864	174,400	36,408,892	41,824	132,585	76.02%	Houston	Houston

The next step is to identify the crossover thresholds for the 80/20 distribution. Find the row in the worksheet where Cumulative Current Year Sales equals 80% of Total Current Year Sales. Set the color of the Current Year Sales cell in this row and all the rows above it to Green. Next, find the row where Cumulative Current Year Sales equals 95% of Total Current Year Sales. Set the color of the Current Year Sales cell in this row and all the rows above it up to the last cell colored Green to Yellow. Finally, set the color of the Current Year Sales cells in the remaining rows to Red. The resulting worksheet should now look like:

The top rows of the worksheet are the customers who account for 80% of Current Year Sales. The middle block plus the top block account for 95% of Current Year Sales. The final block, which will likely extend for several more pages, represent what is generally the largest number of customers. Although this third list is long, it only accounts for the last 5% of Current Year Sales.

When you've completed the process for Current Year Sales, the next step is to repeat the effort using Current Year Margin. Start by sorting the worksheet from highest to lowest on the Current Year Margin column. Then, insert a new column, Cumulative Margin, to calculate a running total of Current Year Margin. Using the Cumulative Margin column, locate the 80/20 and 95/5 crossover thresholds and set the cell colors in the Current Year Margin column to Green, Yellow, or Red in the same manner that you color-coded the Current Year Sales cells in the worksheet. The result will be a worksheet with color-coding in two columns:

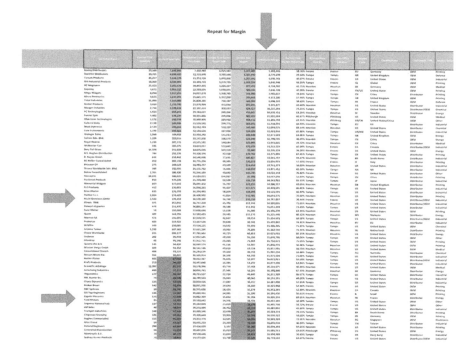

Repeat for Margin

You may notice that some of the cells in the Cumulative Current Year Sales column report errors of one sort or another. This is an unavoidable artifact that results from analyzing two columns containing running totals in the same worksheet.

Once you've completed the analysis with the customer worksheet, repeat the process with the product worksheet.

CREATING THE QUAD MAP FROM THE TRANSACTION FILE

The transaction file is typically quite large; consequently, we only look at the most recent 12 months. However, if you notice a major shift from the other files then you will want to go back and capture this data.

Within your transaction file, you have your customers and the products that they purchase.

Based on the results of the 80/20 analysis, you want to classify customers as either top 20% or bottom 80%. You classify products in the same way. Once classified, you summarize the transaction data by quadrant.

STEP ONE

- Open the 80/20 customer file/tab.

- Insert a new column for CUSTOMER CLASSIFICATION.

- For all customers above the Crossover Threshold (i.e. The 20% of customers accounting for 80% of gross margin), set the value of CUSTOMER CLASSIFICATION to "1".

- For all customers below the Crossover Threshold (i.e. The 80% of customers accounting for the remaining 20% of gross margin), set the value of CUSTOMER CLASSIFICATION to "2".

STEP TWO

- Open the 80/20 product file/tab.

- Insert a new column for PRODUCT CLASSIFICATION.

- For all customers above the Crossover Threshold (i.e. The 20% of products accounting for 80% of gross margin), set the value of PRODUCT CLASSIFICATION to "1".

- For all customers below the Crossover Threshold (i.e. The 80% of products accounting for the remaining 20% of gross margin), set the value of PRODUCT CLASSIFICATION to "2".

STEP THREE

- Open the transaction file/tab.

- Insert a new column for CUSTOMER CLASSIFICATION.

- Insert a new column for PRODUCT CLASSIFICATION.

- Using a Vlookup, retrieve the appropriate CUSTOMER or PRODUCT CLASSIFICATION from the customer and product files for each line in the transaction file.

- Set the value of CUSTOMER CLASSIFICATION and PRODUCT CLASSIFICATION appropriately for each line in the transaction file.

STEP FOUR

- Open/continue with the transaction file/tab.

- Insert a new column for QUAD ASSIGNMENT

- Assign transaction lines to quads using the following rules:

- ○ If Customer is 1 and the Product is 1 – assign transaction line to Quad 1.

- ○ If Customer is 1 and the Product is 2 – assign transaction line to Quad 2.

- ○ If Customer is 2 and the Product is 1 – assign transaction line to Quad 3.

- ○ If Customer is 2 and the Product is 2 – assign transaction line to Quad 4.

- Summarize total revenue, total gross margin, number of customers, and number of products by Quad assignment.

  - ○ Filter the transaction worksheet by Quad number (displaying only those transactions classified as belonging to Quad 1, for example)

  - ○ Calculate total revenue and total gross margin

  - ○ Count the number of unique customers and products (use the Remove Duplicates command in Excel)

- Summarize the final results into a single Quad Analysis Table

EXAMPLES OF EXCEL COMMANDS USED IN THE PROCESS

- Calculation of the product quad number assigning either a 1 or 2 to the Product Quad Number.

  - ○ =VLOOKUP(#REF!, 'Product Quad Number'!$A$1:$B$2481,2,TRUE)

- Calculation of the customer quad number assigning either a 1 or 2 to the Customer Quad Number.

  - ○ =VLOOKUP(CLEAN(TRIM(D3)),'Customer Quad Number'!$A$1:$AH$241,2,TRUE)

- Calculation for the determination of the Quad based on the Customer and Product 80/20 classification.

  - ○ =IF(A3+B3=2,1,IF(A3>B3,2, IF(B3>A3,3,4)))

A Hypothetical Quad Analysis

Customers \ Products	20/80 (Top 20% SKUs ~80% of Margin)	80/20 (Remaining 80% ~20% of Margin)	
20/80 (Top 20% customers ~80% of Margin)	**Quad 1** Customers: 75 Products: 20 Sales: $12.8M Margin: $ 5.8M	**Quad 2** Customers: 59 Products: 35 Sales: $ 3.8M Margin: $ 1.4M	79% of Total Margin
80/20 (Remaining 80% ~20% of Margin)	**Quad 3** Customers: 425 Products: 19 Sales: $ 3.2M Margin: $ 1.3M	**Quad 4** Customers: 525 Products: 44 Sales: $ 1.5M Margin: $ 0.5M	21% of Total Margin
	78% of Total Margin	22% of Total Margin	

APPENDIX 3—KANBAN CALCULATIONS

Calculating Kanban size should take into consideration your lead time, daily usage and safety stock. This is a simple calculation of adding these three items together to determine your inventory requirements. The lead time, which represents the time from when you figure out that your bin is empty to the time when you receive the items you reordered, tends to be your largest variable, but there are ways to control this.

When I help other companies develop a full Kanban lean process, I tend to start with a week's worth of supply. One week of Kanban is what would normally be considered perfection. Perfection is a pretty high water mark. However, before you can even come close to perfection you need to implement the Rolling Purchase Order System, Vendor Reduction, Kanban, Pull Through, and C Class techniques discussed in the toolkit.

CALCULATION OF KANBAN QUANTITIES WITHOUT ROLLING PURCHASE ORDER SYSTEM

Take the number of days from the point of ordering, plus days of safe stock, and then multiply this number by the number of parts used per day. This will give you the quantity of parts you should carry in stock.

- Lead Time + Safety Stock = # of Days * Number of Parts Used Per Day   = Kanban

CALCULATION OF KANBAN QUANTITIES WITH ROLLING PURCHASE ORDER SYSTEM

You want to have your vendors supply you with parts within a 5-day time frame from the receipt of an order. This is discussed in detail in the rolling purchase order section. You would then take your annual volume and divide it by 52 (the numbers of weeks in a year) to come up with your Kanban quantities.

- 5 Days + Safety Stock = # of Days * Number of Parts Used Per Day   = Kanban

This is for a two-bin system. If you want to be a little more conservative you can always take the total quantity that you calculate and divide it up into 3 Kanbans. This shifts your inventory trigger from 50% of your available inventory up to 66%, 33% and Zero of your available inventory. If you go to 4 Kanban Cards then you shift the first inventory trigger at 75%, 50%, 25% and Zero of the remaining inventory requirement.

As you shift from 2 to 3 or 4 Kanban Cards – then your order quantities decrease and you have to make certain you are hitting your minimums. You also need to go through and verify that you are purchasing the correct packaging quantity. A good Kanban system will make it easy to manage the inventory and the cards. You don't want a more than 4 cards for an area or you might as well just go to a master bin system where you feed the parts into the line. However, it is always better to have Point of Use if possible.

Keep in mind, however, that this equation is designed for an ideal business organization - one that has a consistent demand of the raw material into the production system, has vendors that are trained and have their items ready to ship to you according to a release system. It is critical that your employees understand the system and have been trained to execute it.

In the beginning work with larger Kanban Systems and figure out how to build some type of automatically reduction system so that as you have the system running you can strip out inventory without resizing everything

APPENDIX 4—VIFREDO PARETO

The concept generally labeled the 80/20 Rule developed from the observations of Italian economist and nobleman Vilfredo Pareto beginning in 1906. Thirteen years after he arrived in Switzerland, he made a groundbreaking observation that would later develop into the Pareto principle. His initial observation focused on the relationship between the Italian land and members of its population - he saw that the relationship was 80/20, respectively. In other words, the wealthiest 20% of the population owned and controlled up to 80% of the land. He went on to study wealth and income in other countries, namely Britain, Germany, Ireland, and Peru, finding an uneven distribution of wealth in all these areas that was largely consistent with his 80/20 finding in 1906. In the case of Britain, the distribution was closer to 70/30, but even so the upper class represented a relatively small group of people who accounted for a large portion of the overall national income. A look at the current distribution of income in the United States today would reveal this pattern as true.

While studies on other world populations, both in Pareto's time and many years later, may reveal some exceptions to this rule, the data supporting Pareto's research cannot be ignored. It has influenced a wide variety of political, social and economic movements. Although Pareto's economic ideas and research garnered widespread support from future economists and scholars, his political views were less popular, even controversial. In his sociological book, Mind and Society (1916), Pareto stressed the unreasoning elements in social life and emphasized the role of leading groups in society. Pareto was a vehement critic of democracy and regarded history as a succession of aristocracies, which led him to pose alternative political ideologies that closely resembled the collective beliefs that came to embody fascism. Some scholars have gone so far as to call him the "ideological father" of Fascism. There is uncertainty as to whether he actually supported the Fascist movement going on in Italy around the time of World War I, but Benito Mussolini, arguably the founder of the Fascism, drew inspiration from Pareto in his rise to power.

Regardless of Pareto's now infamous political views, his studies on wealth distribution and the subsequent 80/20 principle he identified have been applied to a variety of other realms, including American business. The term, "Pareto Principle" was coined by quality consultant Joseph M. Juran. He personally discovered the principle in his late thirties and decided to try applying it to issues of quality, such as how 80% of an individual's problems can be created by 20% of the causes of their problems. Another term that he used to reference the principle was the "law of the vital few and the trivial many." There are many ways that individuals can apply this principle to their everyday lives. Richard Koch authored a book[14] about the principle, documenting its usage in virtually every major aspect of human life. The principle can be quite instrumental in sorting out various problems and tasks that a person may encounter during a day. In using the Pareto principle an individual may be able to remove some of the less important aspects from their attention and focus most on the ones that they deem most essential and vital.

More recently, Pareto's principle has become increasingly relevant in the business world. Multiple companies have operated under the assumption that 80% of their revenue should come from 20% of their customers. Similarly, companies may develop their product lines in such a way that 20% of the products account for up to 80% of the overall business. While some businesses may exhibit this trend naturally, others take it upon themselves to consciously follow the principle and use it as a major strategy for determining how to run their business.

APPENDIX 5—ILLINOIS TOOL WORKS (ITW)

Founded in 1912 by 4 businessmen, Illinois Tool Works' (ITW) product line initially consisted solely of metal-cutting tools. During World I, the company began expanding their product line to include other items of value to the wartime economy, such as truck transmissions and pumps. The Second World War provided more opportunity for ITW to develop new products to aid the war effort. Among these products was the innovative water cutter that sliced into heavy artillery barrels in an efficient, timesaving manner. In this period, the company also made its first effort to decentralize the company and develop a degree of specialization in their overall business. Some of the earlier units were the Fastex unit, which specialized in fasteners; the Licon unit, which specialized in electrical products; and the Spiroid unit, which specialized in metal fabrication. The company acquired its new and current name in the 1960s and formally entered the New York Stock exchange trading under the symbol ITW.

Today, ITW operates as a Fortune 150 company with 850 business units in 52 countries and roughly 60,000 employees. The main industries served by ITW are transportation, industrial packaging, power systems and electronics, food equipment, construction products, polymers and fluids, and decorative surfaces. While the United States accounts for about 43% of the company's total revenue, the company now generates a significant percentage of its revenue from other countries - 31% from Europe, 11% from Asia, 6% from other North American countries, 5% from Oceania, and 4% from South America and Africa. Although the company has made considerable strides in expanding to a larger international base, some risks in lower cost nations, such as political or financial instability, issues with government regulation, and poor adherence to intellectual property rights, have made ITW reluctant to manufacture and do business in these nations.

The company has received attention for its ability to prosper amid a struggling U.S. economy. Forbes reported in October 2011 that the company has been experiencing an average growth rate of 14.5% over the past four quarters. The most recent projection for ITW's overall 2011 revenue is up to $17.92 billion. Investment analysts assert that the company is an attractive stock to invest in. In adapting favorably to an unsettling economic climate, the company raises the question of what drives success in today's business world. A closer look at the company's history, development, and core strategy provides an answer to this inquiry.

The company follows a strategy of cultivating growth within business units until units reach a critical mass and then splitting them into smaller, more specialized units. When these splits occur new units generally end up with their own manufacturing and engineering departments allowing them to function independently, sharing little with their parent company. This model is beneficial to ITW as a whole and to the employees working at each business. In separating their business into many smaller units, the company ensures that each unit is employed and led by individuals with a strong understanding of their specific division or industry, which in turn leads to stronger sales and better insight into customer's needs. Employees also benefit because they have more opportunity to move up in the company and take on a leading role at a younger age. ITW has recently started to review the definition of a small, focused company. They have made some recent changes to increase the target revenue stream for an independent management team. Another core feature of ITW's strategy is their commitment to the 80/20 principle, which observes that 80% of company's profits come from a core 20% of their customers. ITW spends a great deal of time devising strategies to appeal to their 20% core and systematically treats the remaining 80% of their customers differently. For example, top customers are dealt with directly through field sales, while the remaining customers interact largely with distributors. While other businesses make use of this principle, few have had as much success as ITW.

In addition to the 80/20 principle and business segmentation, ITW also emphasizes product line simplification, outsourcing, in-lining and pull-through production as important conceptual tools that contribute to the success of the company. In their annual report for 2005, ITW explicitly credits these tools key factors in their overall success. Product line simplification refers to the process of evaluating products to ensure that the business can better serve their key customers. In evaluating products, it becomes clear which items stand out as top sellers and, consequently, deserve the most attention, and which products are of secondary importance and can be consolidated, outsourced, or even removed from the company's product line altogether. Through in-lining, ITW simplifies manufacturing processes in order to promote greater productivity and revenue increases. Finally, pull-through production is a tool for modeling production off of actual order receipt, rather than an inventory target that doesn't effectively account for patterns and changes in customer demands.

Why would ITW's practices be relevant to a business owner and/or middle management? ITW has spent years learning how to streamline companies and run successfully run businesses. They are very public about the techniques used in their process. ITW has a strong track record built on improving the way medium scale businesses manage and run their operations. There have been many good books written about General Motors, Apple and General Electric, but from a small and medium-scale business perspective, their smallest divisions are 20 times the size of your company. Insights from the giants, while sounding effective and impressive, offer few practical insights for those of us in the middle. Learning from the giants of business is like taking navigating lessons from an aircraft carrier when you are sailing your Sunfish. Other than some broad observations about how big and wet the ocean is, there isn't much insight or practical advice on what to do with a Sunfish.

ITW has fine-tuned the process of sailing 850 different Sunfish all in similar fashions. The interesting fact is that they tend to be successful at sailing in every type of body of water. If you look at the ITW Web-site you will find three basic operating principles. It is clear what is important to them:

- Decentralization.

- 80/20 Process.

- Innovation.

The decentralization process is about pushing management decisions down to the General Manager Level, the 80/20 process is about setting an effective focus within a business and innovation is about not only making new and innovative products, but also about innovating the way business is done.

Marek Ciserenks, is an investment analyst from BMO Harris Bank who studies large, diversified manufacturers.

We talked about the ITW model with Mr. Ciserenks, who observed that it seemed like 850 small business being supported by a larger corporate infrastructure. The 850 business units seemed to have common themes to them. Further, the Corporate Staff is almost non-existent and the revenue per employee is exceptionally high.

We talked about the grass roots approach pushing acquisitions done to the General Manager Level and we spoke about Tim's experience as a General Manager with ITW. The direction from Tim's boss was that we were looking to get the phone call when someone wanted to sell their company. My boss would always tell me that we want to get the phone call before the private equity guys. The key was to be trusted and to build this trust over the years. Marek stated that ITW liked to acquire the business after a major event in an owner's life – such as divorce or death.

The general pitch we would make to an owner was that we would leave the business intact and offer better benefits to the employees. Whether this pitch proved true depended largely on how well a business performed. Marek commented that he was pleased to see the business from the bottom side had the same pitch as the business was presented to analysts.

Marek commented that ITW's investment performance "has been nothing short of spectacular" Since 1989, ITW has returned 1,322.9% vs. 517.5% for the S&P 500 and 578.7% for the S&P Industrial sector, which is a good proxy for ITW's peers. In annualized terms, that's 12.7% on average for 22 years vs. 8.6% for the S&P 500 and 9.0% for the S&P Industrials. All those figures are total return, meaning that is exactly what you as a shareholder would've enjoyed (dividends plus share price appreciation).

Acquisitions also represent an important growth driver for this diversified manufacturer. In fiscal year 2010 the company made almost 25 acquisitions acquiring revenue of over one-half of a billion dollars. In the first quarter of fiscal 2011 they closed an additional six acquisitions generating revenues in excess of $300 million. Illinois Tool Works' goal is to add revenue growth of approximately $1 billion in fiscal year 2011 through acquisitions. In addition to expanding their business into new markets, acquisitions also strengthen their standing in existing markets.

This is a company that has been successful at what it does. Illinois Tool Works (ITW) is a solid growth story with an above-average earnings growth rate. The company also offers a strong dividend yield of 2.8% and a solid capital structure with a debt equity ratio of only 21%.

ITW is a large holding company. ITW is particularly good at purchasing smaller companies and then streamlining them by applying a set of principles. They are surprisingly public about this principles and practices. Their focus has historically been the neglected middle.

There is a story about Jim Farrell, retired President of ITW during the first part of this millennium, where he was presenting the 80/20 principle to a group of business people. After the presentation one of the attendees asked, "if this is so special why are you sharing it so freely?" His comment was that few managers have the discipline to successfully apply it.

ACKNOWLEDGEMENTS

As with any effort of this scale, many hands went into its creation. Stuart Miller of Colonnade Advisors suggested that we combine our efforts in another example of his talent for recognizing opportunities well before others can see them. Stuart also provided feedback and insight as the effort and the manuscript evolved. Elizabeth Ritter and Andrea Yelin provided research and editorial support early on and throughout the effort. Marek Ciserenks of BMO Harris Bank helped us understand how the market views and values ITW.

Many busy executives, whose calendars were already overfull, made time to read and review the manuscript including Claude Demby, Bob Kocis, Alex Schroeder, Mike Sellers, Tom Siebrasse, Dave Snyder, John Vlahakis, John Wengler, and Charlie Wise. Their candor and low tolerance for fuzzy thinking helped us and the manuscript greatly. Any residual fuzziness is our doing.

We would also like to acknowledge our clients and employers over the years. They've taught each of us much about how to be more effective at analyzing complex situations and making effective improvements. Sometimes, the lessons have been more along the lines of "don't ever try that again." Whatever the lesson, we have chosen not to identify specific clients by name, nor have we linked our examples to our individual paths.

Mary Ward has an extraordinary design eye and we took full advantage of it.

Writing, whether with pen and paper or keyboard and laptop, takes place in many settings and we took advantage of most of them. We do want to thank both Caribou Coffee and Starbucks Coffee in Winnetka, Illinois for their hospitality as our conference rooms and meeting spaces.

Finally, our wives, Mary Nelson and Charlotte McGee tolerated and supported our efforts as they have many times before. They hardly ever laughed when we told them we were done the first dozen times.

ABOUT THE AUTHORS

Tim Nelson

Tim graduated Cum Laude from San Diego State University with a BS with Distinction in Finance and then spent several years working in various finance roles for several large organizations. He received his MBA from the University of Chicago specializing in Operations and Accounting. Tim founded Midwest Industrial Packaging, Inc. (MIP) in 1987, which was sold to Illinois Tool Works (ITW) in 2000. Spent seven years as Vice President and General Manager for ITW helping to manage and improve several divisions. In 2008, he founded a new packaging equipment company while performing consulting projects leading transformational projects to improve businesses ranging from $50 million to $100 million in revenue. He has helped transform multiple business units utilizing the techniques and processes discussed in the book.

Jim McGee

Jim was one of the Founding Partners of Diamond Management & Technology Consultants in 1994, helping it grow from 25 employees in 1994 to over 1,000 consultants and $260 million in revenue in 2000. He has also worked as a consultant and entrepreneur with Accenture, Huron Consulting Group, Ernst & Young, and Collaborating Minds. Jim has taught organizational design, organizational change, technology management, strategy, and economics at Northwestern's Kellogg School of Management, DePaul University's School for New Learning, and Columbia College of Chicago. Jim has a BA in Statistics from Princeton University, an MBA in Strategy from the Harvard Business School, and a Doctorate in Organizational Design, also from the Harvard Business School.

How our collaboration began

The collaboration that produced this book began with a conversation at a Christmas party. A friend suggested that we meet to investigate the overlap in our backgrounds and interests. Our lives had already intersected in several ways in the community where we live. In the mid-1990s, Jim coached one of Tim's children in AYSO soccer. Our wives play in the Handbell Choir at our church. What we hadn't previously done was compare notes on our professional backgrounds and experiences.

Tim used the long flights between Chicago and North Carolina to mine his experiences using the tools and practices he had learned, developed, and honed during his time at ITW. During this time, he produced an early version of the manuscript at the core of this book. The approach always produced excellent results when properly implemented. Tim struggled to understand three questions:

- Why weren't more organizations routinely doing 80/20 analysis?

- Why were organizations reluctant to implement the seemingly simple changes needed to reap clear rewards?

- Why were the straightforward tools and techniques he had learned not taught, while more esoteric concepts with limited application filled classes, seminars, workshops, and journals?

Jim, meanwhile, had again crossed the boundary between practice and theory and was teaching a newly designed graduate course on understanding personal and organizational change. After multiple roles as systems designer, programmer, database designer, project manager, strategy consultant, teacher, researcher, organizational designer, and entrepreneur, Jim was asking a related set of questions:

- How is the practice of organizational change evolving where change is now the norm rather than the exception in today's competitive, dynamic, and global, economy?

- Why are organizations slow to adopt and adapt new knowledge about using data and information to make more effective decisions?

- How do you connect insights to sustained, effective, action in complex organizations?

Our unique mix of interests and experience led us to tackle these questions from a pragmatic perspective. The changing economics of data processing and software technology make the tools for this work affordable and accessible to organizations of virtually any scale. And the essence of connecting insight to action depends on effectively engaging those with the power to implement change to the process of developing insights from the evidence.

The tools in this book and the insights you gain from the process will enable you and your organization to identify, cultivate, develop, and implement the changes necessary to create increased value within your organization.

ON THE WEB

Some of the exhibits and examples we use in the book are fairly complex. Full-size, high-resolution versions of the exhibits and examples can be found at www.insidethe8020box.com/resources.

If you discover errors or have suggestions on how we might improve the book, please visit www.insidethe8020box.com/feedback, or send an email to feedback@insidethe8020box.com.

Finally, you can find new information on applying and extending the methods and techniques in this book at www.insidethe8020box.com.

NOTES

[1] . "Vilfredo Pareto: The Concise Encyclopedia of Economics, Library of Economics and Liberty", accessed March 31, 2013. http://www.econlib.org/library/Enc/bios/Pareto.html.

[2] . U.S. Small Business Administration Office of Advocacy. "Frequently Asked Questions About Small Business", September 2012.

[3] ·· Private Equity Growth Capital Council. "Private Equity by the Numbers", August 2012. http://www.pegcc.org/education/pe-by-the-numbers/.

[4] ·· "Private Equity Invests $144 Billion in 1,702 U.S. Companies in 2011 - Private Equity Growth Capital Council", accessed March 31, 2013. http://www.pegcc.org/newsroom/press-releases/private-equity-invests-144-billion-in-1702-u-s-companies-in-2011/.

[5] · Welch, Jack, and Suzy Welch. *Winning.* HarperCollins, 2005.

[6] · "*The War of the Worlds* (radio Drama)." *Wikipedia, the Free Encyclopedia,* November 19, 2012. http://en.wikipedia.org/w/index.php?title=The_War_of_the_Worlds_(radio_drama)&oldid=523769911.

[7] . Christensen, Clayton M. *The Innovator's Dilemma.* Harvard Business School Pr, 1996.

[8] Vaill, Peter B. *Learning As a Way of Being: Strategies for Survival in a World of Permanent White Water.* Jossey-Bass, 1995.

[9] Boland, "450 Billion Oreos to Go." *New York Times.* July 28, 2002

[10] Nobelprize.org. "Herbert A. Simon - Autobiography", 1978. http://www.nobelprize.org/nobel_prizes/economics/laureates/1978/simon-autobio.html.

[11] Mariotti, John L. *The Complexity Crisis: Why Too Many Products, Markets, and Customers Are Crippling Your Company--and What to Do About It.* Adams Media, 2008.

[12] Rogers, Everett M. *Diffusion of Innovations.* 4th ed. Free Press, 1994.

---

[13] "Harold Geneen - Wikipedia, the Free Encyclopedia", accessed March 31, 2013. http://en.wikipedia.org/wiki/Harold_Geneen.

[14] Koch, Richard. *The 80/20 Principle : The Secret of Achieving More With Less*. Bantam Doubleday Dell Pub (Trd), 1998.